Visual Programming

Crucial Study Texts for Computing Degree Courses

Titles in the series

To order, please call our order line 0845 230 9000, or email orders@learningmatters.co.uk, or visit our website www.learningmatters.co.uk

Visual Programing

David J. Leigh

**Computing series editor:
Peter Hodson**

First published in 2003 by Crucial, a division of Learning Matters Ltd.

© David Leigh

British Library Cataloguing in Publication Data
A CIP record for this book is available from the British Library.

ISBN 1 903337 11 9

Cover design by Topics – The Creative Partnership
Project management by Deer Park Productions
Text design by Code 5 Design
Typeset by PDQ Typesetting, Newcastle under Lyme
Printed and bound by Bell & Bain Ltd, Glasgow

Learning Matters Ltd
33 Southernhay East
Exeter EX1 1NX
Tel: 01392 215560
Email: info@learningmatters.co.uk
www.learningmatters.co.uk

Contents

Dedication

This book is dedicated to my friends pictured within.

Introduction
Visual Programming

Which courses this book covers

This guide is intended to assist students who are improving their programming skills. It is assumed that some programming knowledge and skills have already been gained. The previous language used is not specifically important.

It can be used alone or as part of formal studies. It is, above all, an outline. It cannot substitute for a reference guide to a Visual Programming language. It introduces particular concepts associated with Visual Programming based on the language Visual Basic. These are transferable to other languages, but the methods and language syntax used are specific.

It is founded firmly on the concept of 'learning by doing'. Theoretical knowledge and practical skills are presented in parallel. Each is intended to reinforce the other.

It is assessed in two ways. One is by a mixture of questions which can be answered orally or (more probably) in written form. The other is by the solution of practical programming problems. These will require further (written) documentation to describe the design processes used. They will also include in-line documentation included with the program code.

Courses covered by this guide will therefore probably be placed in the second half of a first-year undergraduate programme, or at the beginning of the second year. Such courses will probably include 'Visual Programming' or 'Visual Basic' in their title. This may be qualified by 'Introduction to' or have suffix 'I'.

The programme of study may be for Edexcel BTEC Higher National Certificate or Diploma, where this work corresponds to Unit 15 (Visual Programming). However, more material is presented in this guide than is specifically defined in the Edexcel defining document for that unit. The work also applies fully to degree-level studies, which are defined by each university according to its own curriculum and requirements.

Layout of the book

Each chapter follows the same format. This introductory part contains a summary of the contents, a list of learning outcomes, and the methods of assessment used on the subject matter. Each chapter section is introduced by a summary, and followed by quick questions on the chapter contents. The chapters close with examples and answers, followed by a list of references.

Learning outcomes have been widely adopted to describe what a student should gain by studying on an academic course. They have been adopted here for a similar purpose. They form a checklist of the expectations of each chapter. They should be used actively to ensure that they have been met in each case.

They may be combined to form an overall set for the guide as a whole. These may be summarised in a concise form so that, following successful completion of this study guide, a student should be able to:

- design and implement simple applications in a Visual Programming language;
- use a suitable Program Development Environment;
- test the applications developed to demonstrate that they correspond to their specifications;
- document and present the applications to allow their maintenance;
- amend existing applications for maintenance purposes;
- follow suitable Software Engineering construction principles.

The **methods of assessment** are described using key words to indicate the ways in which questions can be asked or tasks set about each chapter. Among these, you will find the following. **Describe** indicates that this can be done as an oral or written test, perhaps in multiple-choice format. **Discuss** is similar, but expects greater insight into the operations being carried out. **Demonstrate** is used when the assessment may be either written or 'hands on', or submitted as a report or as a program file. **Write** (as in 'write a program') will usually expect a fully tested and working application, probably with design work included. **Implement** means that a working application is expected.

Planning your study

The learning outcomes will help you in the strategy of your studies. You can set longer-term goals for your work, and check that they have been carried out in this way.

In more immediate terms, a number of ways have been included to help you learn. The most obvious are the **quick questions** at the end of each section. Do not avoid them, but write down the answers. If necessary, check back to make sure that you understand why **these** questions are asked in **this** place. These are backed up by questions at the end of each chapter, with suggested answers. These answers are **not** always complete. If you find other aspects covered by them, write those down as well. Do **not** glance at the questions and the short solutions, and accept that you necessarily understand. Write down your own solutions, and check them.

Throughout the guide there are also tips, concepts and activities. Make a note of the tips, and make sure that you understand the concepts. Write these down also, with any other material which applies to the concept area. Most importantly, carry out the activities and write down what you have done. If anything goes wrong, write that down also, and the steps needed to correct it. In that way, next time a similar error occurs, you have the solution already attached to the problem description.

It is suggested that learning typically takes effect by listening and seeing; by writing; and by doing. The first category is usually at about the 20% level (we remember about one-fifth of what we see and hear under normal circumstances). This doubles to about 40% when it is written down, because there is activity associated with the learning. This doubles again (at least) to about 90% when more formal activity is involved, particularly of the kind involved when an application is developed.

The message should be clear. If you really want to learn from this guide, you will be undertaking quite a lot of writing of one kind and another. Use a log book. Make indexes as you need them. Keep it organised.

What's in the book

Why is Visual Programming of interest? Much of the day-to-day work carried out using a computer system now relies on aspects of Visual Programming so that its users can take advantage of the applications supplied. It is constructed from a number of standard building blocks, called **controls**.

The development of this book is largely based around those different controls used in Visual Programming. These are the components which comprise a Visual Program. Each has its own characteristics, and to gain the best outcomes you will need to be acquainted with them all.

There are others. This guide is just that: a guide. As it says above, this is not a reference book. There is not enough room for that. It will, however, provide a map of the territory of Visual Programming. It is good enough to plan a route, without showing all of the detailed paths.

There are other aspects to help in the learning process. There is a certain amount of repetition, to assist in the reinforcement of the concepts and applications to be studied. There are elements of external context, forming the framework in which Visual Programming exists. There are tools introduced to help with the work to be done. Not all of this is explicit: some of it appears as no more than a reference.

Chapter 1
Structure and approach

Chapter summary

This chapter tells you what to expect from this book on Visual Programming. It will allow you to check that you are following the correct approaches to your learning.

Learning outcomes

The learning outcomes of this chapter aim to ensure that you are reading the correct book. You should be able to:

Outcome 1: Make sure that language you will be learning is the one you want to learn.

Outcome 2: Appreciate different techniques for learning the language.

Outcome 3: Understand the different types of programming involved.

Outcome 4: Appreciate the approaches to be taken with Visual Programming.

How will you be assessed on this?

This is not really an area for direct assessment. Rather, it is for self-assessment to ensure that this is the subject area that you wish to be working on.

Section 1

Welcome – take an active approach

In this section you are being reminded about expected prior knowledge and experience.

You have opened this book because you want to improve your understanding of Visual Programming, and your programming skills. At least, that is what is hoped for. Welcome the opportunities, and enjoy the experience. It is designed to assist you, not only in the programming aspects you already know, but also in extending the use of those aspects in a practical way.

This involves a choice at the very beginning. There are many programming languages which could have been used; but to make the learning easier and to avoid confusion, one alone has been selected for this book. This is Visual Basic. It has been chosen because it is easily available, it is widely used, and it has a good integrated support system. It also provides straightforward pathways into the learning and uses of other languages.

You are not expected merely to read the book, but to learn by carrying out actual tasks. These are not always graded in terms of increasing complexity, but many will build on lessons learnt before. This means that you will not be a passive participant, but will be active in your approach. You will develop your competence by **doing** – which is the only real way of making practically-based abilities work.

You will carry out tasks of two different kinds: theoretical, to increase your knowledge; and practical, to increase your skills. You need to do both to get the best results. You will find that some are easier than others, and that the levels of difficulty will depend on what you are being asked to do. Some but not all of the theoretical parts are signalled by the phrase **crucial concept**. Pay particular attention to these, because they have been picked out as important to the subject area. (You will also find a **crucial tip** in some places – that means what it says, and should smooth your learning as long as you pay attention to it.)

Some of the practical work is quite short, but you should tackle it at the place it appears. For this you will need access to a computer system using Visual Basic©. The examples given are from Visual Basic version 6.0, running under Windows 2000©. But if you are using a different operating system or another release of Visual Basic, you will not find it difficult to allow for the changes.

It is assumed that you can run applications (such as Visual Basic) from within your chosen operating system. It is also assumed that you have some familiarity with procedural programming (for instance Pascal, Java, C and so on). The background to the book assumes that you know about the kinds of variables typically available. These will include integers, real (or floating) numbers, strings (and characters) and so on. It also assumes that you are familiar with the ways in which statements are put together: in **sequences**, or chosen by **selection** (typically using keywords such as `if`), or **iterated** in loops (using keywords such as `for` and `while`).

CRUCIAL TIP

If you are not sure about the above, it would be as well to check your progress very carefully and to get practice in their use before proceeding too far with this book.

The 'knowledge' part of the book is intended to increase and direct your vocabulary in the words and concepts used in Visual Programming. Many of the ideas will be familiar, but it might be necessary to adjust them to work in a new area. These ideas will be integrated with the practical components of your work, so that each aspect progresses in parallel with the other. This means that you must not neglect either aspect, but keep them working together all the way.

CRUCIAL ACTIVITY

Make sure that Visual Basic is the language you want to study. If this is not what you want, *now* is the time to stop.

It is, however, important to realise that Visual Basic does not rely purely on procedural programming. It is a language suited for event-driven activities. This requires a slightly different approach to that used in pure procedural languages. This will be explained and clarified in the following chapters.

CRUCIAL CONCEPT

Visual Basic is a programming language designed to realise event-driven systems.

A word of warning. There is not enough room in this book to explore every aspect of the subject in depth. In many cases, examples will be illustrated with no more than sufficient detail to allow you to undertake further exploration on your own. You should take the opportunity in each case to follow the active learning approach to clarify and extend the foundation presented.

For each chapter, at least one reference is suggested for further study. There are many possibilities, but one must start somewhere. The references to World-Wide Web pages, starting with http://, were working when the book was prepared. Such references can go out of date, so if these 'disappear', you may need to use a search engine to find current information. A word of warning: there is little censorship or regulation applied to such pages. They do not have to be correct. But most of them are reasonable.

Quick test

1. What is the difference between **selection** and **iteration**?

2. Distinguish between **skills** and **knowledge**.

Four threads

This section deals with the production of programs carried out in an efficient way. It distinguishes between four aspects of the implementation process and production. It reinforces matter already known and introduces content and an approach to be used throughout the book.

The structure of this book is organised on a basis of four threads. They will be developed together, and receive more or less emphasis throughout, according to the requirements of each section. They are: the **development environment**; the **language facilities**; the **design, implementation and testing** work; and the associated **application areas**.

Development Environment

This is a set of programs which are (generally) transparent to the programmer. They are intended to support all of the work used in developing and testing a Visual Program within the computer environment, without getting in the way. In other words, if all is going well, they will not even be obvious.

However, if anything appears to be going wrong, or if any help is needed, the Development Environment will step in as an assistant. It is not intended to get in the way at all: if you feel this is happening to you, you should review your own approach and your work carefully. Any message or warning from the Development Environment is intended to correct a situation which it 'believes' may lead to a problem, immediately or in the future.

It is **only** a computer program. Such things are **not** infallible. But experience has shown that warnings from the Development Environment can be important in informing programmers of possible difficulties at an earlier, rather than a later, stage of a program's activities.

CRUCIAL TIP

All computer programs are fallible.

Because the Development Environment is only a program, it will not react to every mistake. If, for example, the wrong variable name is specified in an expression, it cannot guess which the right one ought to have been. It may be able to help – but cannot always – if the wrong type has been specified for a variable (for instance, **integer** for **float**, or *vice-versa*). It is always safer to be cautious and self-critical, because the later that any errors are allowed to persist in a program's development, the harder they are to correct safely.

The Development Environment can be helpful in other`ways. It can allow the values of specified variables to be displayed, on a running basis, while a program is being tested. This Development Environment-based testing may take place a statement at a time, or a routine at a time. It may run to a given statement, to discover whether the correct execution paths are being taken. If variables have not taken the expected values, these may be changed – on an experimental basis only: be careful – to assist in further development.

But it is always present while the Visual Basic program is being developed. That accounts, really, for its name. When the program is in production, the Development Environment is discarded because there is no longer any need for it. (If you believe this not to be true, you should ask yourself why – be truthful – and consider what this implies.) There is no profit in including large portions of program code when they will be of no further use. But while it is needed it can be very useful indeed (the author will not use the word 'essential', but...).

Language facilities

The programming aspects of Visual Basic allow procedural programs to be written in ways with which you are already familiar. But if that were all you wished to do in Visual Programming, it would be avoiding many of the opportunities on offer. It is, then, with the extensions provided by Visual Basic to earlier languages (for instance, Basic) that this book is mainly interested.

It will be necessary to ensure that those familiar fundamental aspects needed here will be properly dealt with. As an example, consider a series of commands designed to find the larger of two numbers, x and y. If the language had a **maximum** function (called max), the statement

```
z = max (x, y)
```

will work. But if the function had not been supplied or written, a suitable equivalent Visual Basic statement is

```
if x > y then
        z = x
    else
        z = y
    endif
```

The layout of this selection statement is not critical to its successful execution. But it is good practice to put separate sub-statements on different lines, and to indent them. This makes it easier to appreciate the program structure. Compare the layout above with

```
if x > y then z = x else z = y endif
```

With such a short example, there is little gain. But if there had been lengthy calculations in each part of the selection, it would have been a different story.

CRUCIAL CONCEPT

Good program layout has a very positive effect on 'understandability'.

There are other ways in which programs may be made more understandable. A convention used in the naming of variables will be explained in Chapter 6. It will be used before that point, but will not create any problems. The use of the convention is purposefully transparent.

Design, implementation and testing

Integrated with the language facility provided by Visual Basic, but separate from it, are the ways in which programs are developed. There are essentially three phases of this development, once a program has been specified.

First, each element of the specification has to be understood and converted into a set of instructions to be carried out. These may vary from program to program and from system to system. They may be long or short, simple or complex. The instructions will probably not be in the programming language to be used – they may be in words, or presented as diagrams. They will represent the design of the required program.

While this design is being constructed, it is a good opportunity to work out how it is to be tested. Are there any specific situations which the program has to cope with? If so, *now* is the time to work out how (expected or forbidden values of variables, permitted or forbidden sequences of execution) to check that these are correct. Include the checking in the design – words or diagrams – to help with later work.

Second, after design comes implementation. The program statements derived from the design have to be constructed in a way understandable to the computer systems and in the chosen language. They may be constructed as a whole and then input, or it may be preferable to carry this out in carefully chosen sections.

In either case, it is important to remember to include in-line documentation or comments. This must be done at the same time as the program is implemented and input.

CRUCIAL TIP

Doing the correct thing at the correct time saves a lot of trouble. There is **no** exception to this.

Third, the resulting program must be tested. Test data should be presented to the program to ensure that all possible situations produce the correct response. In an event-driven system, not all data are represented by values of variables. The kind of events and their sequence also form part of the test data. This does not make the planning of tests any more complex. As all testing should be planned and documented in advance, this is merely a different aspect of a well-understood activity.

CRUCIAL CONCEPT

Testing can demonstrate the presence of errors. Testing *cannot* demonstrate a program's complete correctness.

Associated applications

It is not effective, while learning, only to work theoretically in a practical-based subject. As noted above, this book expects an active approach. Therefore each new concept will be attended with practical tasks to be carried out. These will sometimes be given almost in their entirety, and sometimes as an outline only. There may be a tendency to skip some of the former as 'too easy' and not worthy of consideration. The latter may be seen as 'too hard', with an intention of returning to them at a later time when more material has been covered.

Do not take either of these paths. Simple exercises quickly lead to larger ones, and without a secure foundation those larger ones may not succeed. In fact, they are the very ones which might be perceived as 'too hard' if the 'too easy' ones have not been done.

The approach using associated exercises should therefore be followed. These exercises have all been checked by designing, implementing and testing them. In most cases, they have not been made up especially for this book. They represent work actually undertaken, but in many instances the surrounding details have been removed. This has left only that part of the program which illustrates the point being considered.

These applications will not be signalled in any particular way, but will simply form part of the explanation and work to be done. Visual Programming is not a subject which differs from everything else there is, and so the work it is expected to carry out forms part of a computer user's normal activities. In one or two places, you will see the phrase **crucial activity**. That is where there is work to be carried out, and that is the place and time to do it. The most effective ways of learning have been shown to be associated with active participation.

But it does not mean that there is no other work to be done. When you come to any part expecting you to do something, such as questions found at the end of each section, do it then. And write it down. That has a multiple purpose. You will remember your work better by the very act of writing something down. And you will also have something to refer back to at a later stage, when you are checking your own subject understanding.

You will also find that Visual Basic instructions appear in other applications. This may appear peculiar, but because Visual Programming routines form a strong foundation for many approaches, it is not so strange after all. These areas will be introduced in Chapter 7, and you will then – the author is sure – start noticing many others. It is enough initially to observe that any powerful tool may be used in many ways.

Quick test

1. How does the layout of a program affect its execution?
2. How (and when) should testing be planned?

Program representation

You will learn how a Visual Basic program is stored, and why this approach has been taken.

Visual Programming using Visual Basic is actually text based, even though the foundation of its ideas relies more obviously on the visual aspects of the work being done. For each picture, or movement made, or window defined (and so on) there is a corresponding piece of text. In some cases this may be quite short – a few lines at most – but in others a seemingly simple activity may produce tens or even hundreds of lines of code.

In fact, this textual foundation should not be particularly unexpected. Before anything may be input to a computer system for processing, it must be in an appropriate form. The choice of that form, and the ways in which input must be processed subsequently, will depend on the work to be done. For a variety of reasons, including transportability, ease of use and efficiency – as well as historical ones – a text basis has been selected for Visual Basic. As a professional programmer, you will need to be aware of this; but you will find that the systems available to you will make their production easy.

This is a strength and a weakness – it means that you do not have to concern yourself with all of the minute details of what is happening while you are producing your Visual Programs. But it also means that if you do not take care to make sure of what is happening at each stage – and to make a careful note of it – it may make later stages of development unnecessarily difficult, or even wrong.

The Development Environment used is an example of where such difficulties may arise. The ease with which new elements of a Visual Program may be created, and the ease with which they can then be changed, leads to rapid and easy implementation. It can be so easy to prepare even complex structures that seemingly insignificant components can easily be forgotten if not noted at the time they are called into being. But if such structures are to be reorganised at a later time, and part of them is ignored, it is not possible to predict the outcomes. That is not a desirable situation at all.

Therefore, much of the time you will be developing programs stretching over many pages of text, but with most of that text being written for you automatically. However, you will be able to inspect the programs at any level of detail you choose, assisted by powerful development tools and interfaces.

This book will work at the appropriate level of detail wherever it happens to be: but if you wish to look 'behind the scenes' at any time, the information will always be there. Sometimes it will be possible to look at the same item in (at least) three ways – as it will appear when actually in use, as it will appear whilst you are developing it, and at the fundamental text level which Visual Basic actually uses. You could, of course, ignore any of these at any particular time: but developing a professional understanding of how these fit together is an important part of what this book aims to do.

The most 'traditional' way of thinking about a part of a Visual Program is as a picture. An example of this is shown in Figures 1.1 and 1.2. To emphasise the point, the object chosen is a picture. There is little difference between the two, which demonstrates the strong connection between the finished product and the way in which it appears during development.

Figure 1.1 Visual representation

However, the way in which the computer system represents these pictures relies on their storage and their expected appearance. These details are stored as text, which is shown below. The size of the picture (its Height and Width) is shown, as is its position (Left and Top), together with other relevant information. There are other items which are needed by the Visual Basic system; but in particular notice the keywords Begin and End. These are typical of many programming languages, and appear here once again.

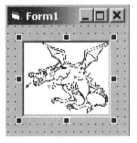

Figure 1.2 Development layout

```
Begin VB.PictureBox Picture1
      Height          =    1215
      Left            =    240
      Picture         =    "Form1.frx":0000
      ScaleHeight     =    1155
      ScaleWidth      =    1395
      TabIndex        =    0
      Top             =    240
      Width           =    1455
   End
```

Because these viewpoints are all representations of the same objects, any view may be used to edit the corresponding part of the visual program. At any one time, however, one of them will probably be better suited for the amendments than the others. A simple example is to be found in the alignment of different parts of the program. While it is possible to be reasonably accurate using one's eyes and a mouse, a more certain way of ensuring that the top left-hand corner of one of the parts is in a particular position is to specify it using its grid reference. This is easy to carry out in Visual Basic. In the example above, Left and Top could be changed in the text representation to ensure that precise and consistent positioning could be provided throughout the Visual Program.

The important outcome is that you are enabled to work efficiently and accurately to produce Visual Programs. They will work, they will be guaranteed and they will be straightforward to change if the need arises. You will be able to pass on such secure programs to others with confidence in a job well done, and to receive such programs from colleagues with similar confidence.

Quick test

1. In what format is a Visual Program stored?

2. How is a Visual Program typically edited?

Visual objects

In this section, some familiar types of Visual Basic components will be discussed.

Visual Objects are the components of a Visual Program. They are joined together to provide the desired effect, whatever that may be. Many of these will already be familiar to you, as they appear in many places within a Windows environment. An example of such a component is the horizontal slider bar shown in Figure 1.3. It is a common inclusion in any Visual Program where not all of the contents of a window will fit into the space available.

Figure 1.3 Horizontal slider bar

─── CRUCIAL ACTIVITY ───

Look at a set of Windows programs and see how many common components you can identify. (Hint: you should find at least ten, and there are more.)

These components may be static, and have no effect on the Visual Program other than to improve its visual aspect and understandability (the example in Figure 1.1 is of this type). They may be dynamic and have an effect on the way in which the program operates – the slider bar shown above is of this kind. In both cases, there is associated Visual Basic code. It is probable that the code for a static component will be entirely generated by the Visual Basic system; but for dynamic components this will be more the responsibility of the programmer.

Within the Visual Basic environment, such components are selected from a menu or from a toolbar. Each one is then edited to have the precise effect wanted by the program in which it is used. This does not affect whether it is static or dynamic in nature. The appearance is largely, but not exclusively, determined in a static way. The effects each one has is typically dealt with by the dynamic aspect.

Such components include forms, text boxes, frames, lists, buttons, and so on. The formal name for these Visual Objects is controls. They are dealt with in further detail in Chapter 2.

Quick test

1. What is the difference between a static and a dynamic activity?

2. How many common components are there in Windows programs?

Section 5

End of chapter assessment

Questions

1. What are the advantages of an active approach to learning?
2. What is a Development Environment?
3. What are three important aspects of program development? What are their characteristics?
4. How are Visual Programs represented within the computer system? How are they presented externally?
5. What are Visual Objects?

Answers

1. The items being learnt are understood more fully, are retained more firmly and are integrated more successfully with students' prior experience.
2. This collection of supporting software assists the production of programs by simplifying the checking of pathways taken and the values of variables during execution. It is also designed to be 'invisible' except when needed.
3. The aspects are design, implementation and testing. The design shows what has to be done when the program is being run; the implementation manages the conversion of that design into instructions understandable to a computer system; and the testing makes sure that the design and the implementation have been successful in realising what was originally required by the program specification.
4. The programs are represented by sequences of text, and may be presented as such. They may also be shown diagrammatically, both during development and execution, according to the requirements of the system and its users.
5. These are the components of a Visual Program, and are combined to create the effects desired by the program specifiers and implementers.

Section 6

Further reading and research

http://msdn.microsoft.com/vbasic/techinfo/articles/ has a large collection of material. It is at many levels, and might best be tackled when you already have some experience. It would not hurt to check what is going on here, though.

Chapter 2
Controls used in
Visual Programming

Chapter summary

This chapter opens with the development environment for constructing Visual Programs, and the code which makes them up. Event-driven systems and the ways in which they may be executed are introduced. Some of the components used are described in more detail, and a simple event-driven Visual Program is constructed.

Learning outcomes

The learning outcomes for this chapter are associated with the development of a simple Visual Program. When you have completed the chapter successfully, you will be able to:

Outcome 1: Describe the environment in which Visual Programs are constructed.
Outcome 2: Describe some of the components which are used in Visual Programs, and their properties.
Outcome 3: Construct a simple Visual Program.
Outcome 4: Discuss simple basic event-driven programming concepts.
Outcome 5: Use ways in which further information can be discovered.
Outcome 6: Describe some Software Engineering principles which apply to Visual Programming.
Outcome 7: Customise the appearance of your Visual Program.

How will you be assessed on this?

You will construct a simple Visual Program. You will be asked questions about the tools and controls used to construct a viable user interface. Some questions will have numerical answers.

Section 1

Building a Visual Program

In this section, you will learn about the environment in which Visual Programs are developed.

To become familiar with Visual Programming – in this case Visual Basic – it will be useful to discover the environment in which it works. So that you can be active in your learning, start by launching the system (as mentioned in Chapter 1, the descriptions and illustrations come from Visual Basic 6.0). You are offered a set of initial choices, shown in Figure 2.1. As this is your first program, open the new Standard EXE option under the *New* tab. (When you access an existing program for maintenance, you will use the *Existing* tab.)

Figure 2.1 Initial choices

The Visual Basic system has opened in Design Mode, and is showing windows for a Project and a Form. The form is the visible part of the Project. (If it is not showing, select *Object* from the *View* menu, or use *Shift-F7*.)

CRUCIAL CONCEPT

Visual Basic is flexible: there is usually more than one way of carrying out any activity in Visual Basic.

Other windows should also be showing: in particular, the Toolbox. If this is not visible (it will look something like Figure 2.2), select *Toolbox* from the *View* menu, or use the **Toolbox** button in the upper toolbar (shown on the right of Figure 2.2). You will need the Toolbox when constructing a Visual Program. It allows you to construct the **controls** described below.

Figure 2.2 Toolbox and Toolbox button

CRUCIAL ACTIVITY

Launch Visual Basic and open the initial Design Mode Project with its form. Make sure the Toolbox is showing.

Quick test

1. Name two ways of displaying the current form in Visual Basic.

2. How many tools are shown in the Toolbox?

Section 2

Visual Programming forms and code

In this section, you will learn about the main component of a Visual Program, the units used for measuring the screens produced, and the way in which program code is stored and displayed.

As an actual Visual Program is being executed, there is a 'Master Component' which is intended to contain all of the others. This allows the components to be placed at picked locations in a controlled way. This component is the **form**, mentioned in Section 1. It is an important part of any Visual Program, and it is possible to produce such a program with no other component. This is not a realistic goal, however: it corresponds to using a computer screen as a single input/output mechanism, with no additional structure. However, to demonstrate the capabilities of a form and the use of some of the associated programming tools, it will be used to show some simple output.

CRUCIAL CONCEPT
The **form** is used in Visual Basic to contain other components.

The appearance of the form in Design Mode shows its actual size, but not necessarily where it will appear when the program is running. The size is also shown on the toolbar, as is the position. The default measuring units used by Visual Basic are called **twips**, although this can be changed. A twip is 1/20 of a printer's point ('**tw**entieth of a **p**oint'), of which 72 make up 1 inch. Thus there are 1,440 twips per inch, and roughly 567 twips per centimetre.

0, 0   4800 x 3600

Figure 2.3 Position and size of form

In Figure 2.3 the top left corner of the form is shown to be at coordinates (0, 0), and the form has a width and height of 4,800 and 3,600 respectively. (That shows the form to be roughly 8½ cm by 6¼ cm in size.) The width and height may be changed by dragging the right side or the bottom of the form. The size display will change accordingly. This will be further explored in Section 7 below.

CRUCIAL CONCEPT
Measurement in Visual Basic is based on the **twip**, which is 1/1440 inch.

Program code is associated with each component of a Visual Program. The active parts are organised into a set of subroutines, which are formally known as **methods.** These methods may be viewed by selecting *Code* from the *View* menu. This opens a window with three components: two small ones above, and a larger one below. The smaller windows, which are known as **combo boxes**, will contain (*General*) on the left, and (*Declarations*) on the right. In the left-hand box, using the arrow, select *Form*. The right-hand box will change to *Load*, and the text

```
Private Sub Form_Load()
End Sub
```

will appear in the larger window component. This is one of the methods which has been prepared in advance for the Visual Programmer. In this case, it is the code to be executed when the form is first set up during the running of the program. There is also a short cut to this code window, by giving a double click in the form in its design view. This is sometimes a more convenient way to access the code. This method will be seen again in Chapter 8, used for initialisation purposes.

CRUCIAL CONCEPT

All Visual Basic is based on **program code** stored as text. The code is organised as a set of **methods.**

The code statements to be executed at this time are inserted between the two lines. These may be (more or less) any valid Visual Basic statements. However, it is reasonable to expect that these would be prepared according to appropriate principles of design, and laid out accordingly. An example of possible code statements to be included in a program is shown below. It will allow for simple output, but will also be used to give an example of parts of a Visual Program which may be included with no extra work from the programmer.

CRUCIAL ACTIVITY

Open the code window and check its contents as described above.

Quick test

1. What does twip stand for? What is the size of a twip in inches? In centimetres?
2. How is program code organised in Visual Basic?

Section 3

A simple event-driven program

In this section, you will be introduced to the organisation and some of the names of a Visual Program's methods. You will also learn how to start and stop the execution of a Visual Program.

Starting from the open code window, the right-hand combo box will show a list of methods which apply to forms. The list is quite a long one, and to see all of the method names a slider is provided to access the entire list. The names are generally self-explanatory: for example, *KeyPress* and *MouseMove*. These methods are called whenever a specific **event** happens which is associated with the form. In the example, the first routine is entered whenever a key (on the keyboard) is pressed; the second is invoked whenever the mouse is moved.

CRUCIAL CONCEPT

Methods are executed in response to **events.**

When the system is initialised, each of these methods is present only as an outline. If any one is selected, its outline code appears in the large window, with the appropriate parameter list in each case. If no code is added, then there is nothing to execute if the given event occurs. It is within these methods, therefore, that code is to be added. For the purpose of this example, simple text will be output whenever the mouse button is used.

This operation is known to the Visual Basic system as a **click**; the associated method for the **form** has the name *Form_Click*. It takes no parameters, as the empty parameter list shows when the method is selected.

CRUCIAL ACTIVITY

Select the **Click** method contained in the form's code. Check the layout of the skeleton code.

The program to be written will consist of a single line of active code, and is inserted after the subroutine heading. However, to ensure good initial programming practice, an explanatory comment will also be added. This will come first, and is introduced, as in many other examples of the Basic language, with an apostrophe. After this, any text can be written on a single line, and will be ignored by the system. (If you prefer, the keyword *Rem* will also introduce a comment.) To distinguish comments, they are given distinctive colours: the default is green. This helps to pick them out from the code statements which are to be executed.

The statement to produce output starts, as in other Basic programs, with the keyword *Print*. The text to be printed is then given as a string of characters, placed within quotation marks. This may be any text at all; a simple message has been selected as an example. When this has been prepared, the program is ready to execute.

```
Private Sub Form_Click()
    ' Output a line each time the mouse button is pressed
    Print "Test message"
End Sub
```

In the same way that comments are presented in a distinctive colour, so are the keywords which are recognised by the Visual Basic system. In the example, the words *Private*, *Sub*, *Print* and *End* all appear with a default colour of dark blue: again, for ease of recognition during program development.

To execute the program, there are three equivalent ways. The command *Start* may be used from the *Run* menu; or the **run** button on the toolbar may be pressed; or the *F5* key may be used. In each case, the form appears in the position specified (see Figure 2.3). However, nothing else happens, because no significant event has taken place. To activate the method, the program must recognise a mouse click associated with the form. As soon as this has been done, the line of text is printed; and this is repeated each time the event takes place.

To stop the program, the command *End* may be used from the *Run* menu; or the **stop** button on the toolbar may be pressed; or the form window may be closed using its associated **close** button in the top right-hand corner. In each case, program execution stops and the form window is closed.

──────── CRUCIAL ACTIVITY ────────

Insert appropriate comments and commands into the skeleton subroutine code. Execute the program.

Quick test

1. Identify five different methods associated with a form.

2. List two ways to start a Visual Basic program.

Section 4

Visual Programming controls

In this section, you will be introduced to different types of Visual Basic components and how they are included in a Visual Program.

In addition to the form, there are several components used in Visual Programming. These components are called **controls**. They should be familiar to users of programs based on windows, and fall into two main groups. Some are intended for the users – **active** controls. Examples of there are **buttons** of different kinds and **text boxes**. These are shown in Figure 2.4.

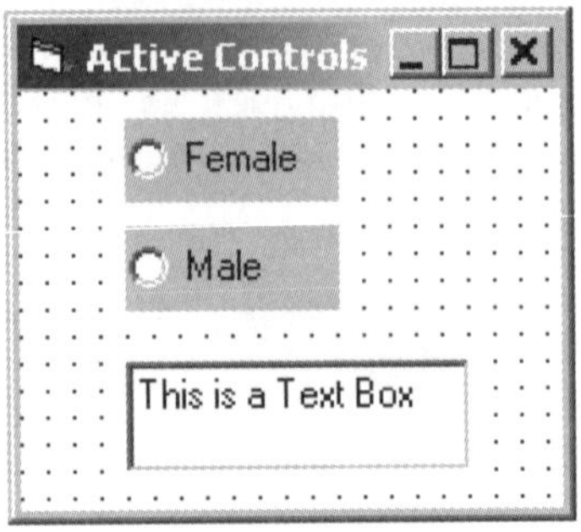

Figure 2.4 Examples of active controls

Others are meant for use by the programs you write, perhaps to give information to users. These are **passive** controls: for instance, pictures and labels. Examples of these are shown in Figure 2.5.

Figure 2.5 Examples of passive controls

CRUCIAL CONCEPT

Visual Programming relies on its **controls**. There are many of these. Some examples are buttons, labels and text boxes.

Active controls are intended for users to interact with. Passive controls are to give information to users. Each kind is set up on the form in the same way, using the toolbox.

The control to be used is selected from the toolbox, using the corresponding button. It is then positioned on the form as a 'drag and drop'. This allows the control's position and size to be specified at the same time. The form is provided with points spaced on a regular grid, to assist with lining controls up in an acceptable pattern. If the control has been positioned or sized incorrectly, it may be moved or resized in the standard way.

CRUCIAL ACTIVITY

Select appropriate controls and place them on the form. If the form becomes too small to hold them, resize it. Adjust the positions and sizes of the controls you have placed on the form.

There are several types of control available to the programmer: 20 are shown in the toolbox in Figure 2.2. It is not proposed to describe them all in detail at this point. They will be introduced, as they are needed, in following sections. Their properties and uses may be found by using the help system, as described in the next section. There may appear to be

21 controls, but the arrow shown in the upper left of Figure 2.2 does not actually define a control. It is an arrow **tool** to help in grouping items. This is dealt with later in the text.

Quick test

1. Name five different Visual Basic controls.

2. How are Visual Basic controls included in a Visual Program?

Use of Visual Basic Help

In this section, you will be introduced to the Help facility included with Visual Basic.

There are many more aspects of Visual Programming, as demonstrated using Visual Basic, than can be shown in this book. It is one of your tasks to use the Visual Basic system to identify these additional aspects, and to learn about them.

You will do this by using the Visual Basic Help facility. This can be started from the *Help* label on the menu bar. You can do this at any time. The result is shown in Figure 2.6.

Figure 2.6 Help screen facility

─── CRUCIAL CONCEPT ───

Visual Basic provides a powerful **Help** facility.

You can see that the initial *Help* drop-down menu has a number of options. Select the *Index* tab and type a subject in the keyword area. This sequence is shown in Figure 2.7, using the keyword 'logical'.

You can also do this directly by using the *F1* key. There are additional facilities made available in this way, as you will find out later.

─── CRUCIAL ACTIVITY ───

Open the Help index, and type 'button' (but without the quotation marks) – or any other word that should apply to Visual Programming. Make a note of what you find out, and how you did it.

─── CRUCIAL TIP ───

You can find out about (nearly) anything in Visual Basic at (almost) any time by using the Help facility.

When you have finished looking anything up, you can minimise (or close) the Help screen in the usual way. You would probably wish to close it if you are sure that you have learnt what you need to know. You might wish to minimise it if it contains a series of steps you need to follow. You can always call it back again when you need it.

If you find something of particular importance, you might want to print the contents of the Help item. You do this most easily using the *Print* icon (circled in Figure 2.7).

Figure 2.7 Help screen in use

CRUCIAL TIP

When you print anything, make sure you keep it safely and well organised. You might also wish to add other (handwritten) notes of your own, such as **what** you were doing at the time, **why** you printed them, and **when** you did it. Your author's notes have headings, dates, and times and sequence numbers on them. They are also filed in a binder.

Never worry about asking for help: it is a good way to start learning. Rudyard Kipling put it very well in *Just So Stories*:

'I keep six honest serving-men
        (They taught me all I knew);
Their names are What and Why and When
        And How and Where and Who.'

Quick test

1. Name two ways of accessing Visual Basic Help.

2. How do you make a printed record of information from the Help system?

Section 6

Visual Programming elements

In this section, you will be introduced to Visual Basic projects and the parts which make them up.

When you are constructing a typical Visual Program, it will consist of a number of different parts. You can develop the parts separately, in a modular fashion. This is usually a good idea anyway. If you develop your work in this way, you can reuse common parts across different applications. This means – apart from less work – that common elements need to be designed, implemented and tested only once.

CRUCIAL CONCEPT

The reuse of common tried-and-tested programming components is one of the fundamentals of **Software Engineering**.

But then, how does a given Visual Program know which parts it is to use? This is done by means of a **project**. This is represented by a file with extension .MAK. Each such file defines the contents of the corresponding program. (For the reasons why this extension is used, you might like to look up the (UNIX) program **make**.)

These items have been carefully organised in a way which makes the most of its host computer's power. For instance, you can execute an existing Visual Program without making any alterations to it. If you then close the Visual Basic system, it will do so without any fuss. But if you make changes and then try to close it down, you will be asked if you want to save those changes (of course, you don't have to if you don't want to). This is part of the work of the project (.MAK) file.

During the next few exercises you will find different project components. Each of these has its particular place inside a project. Therefore, each component will be recorded in the project file. Each different kind is itself held in a file, with a particular extension according to its organisation. If a file has been changed, you will be invited to save that file as the project is closed. This helps to improve the general efficiency of the work being done. No change – no extra work.

To find the contents of a project, look in the project window. This is found as *Project Explorer* on the *View* menu, or from *ctrl-R* on the keyboard. It shows the major project components arranged as a tree. In this way, the dependence of each item on the rest of the structure is readily visible.

Quick test

1. How are the contents of a project displayed?
2. How does Visual Basic use its storage time efficiently?

Section 7

Control properties

In this section, you will be introduced to some of the properties of Visual Basic controls.

There are **properties** associated with each control, and a form also has its own. These define its size, shape, position, colour and many other attributes. Those showing the size and position of the current form have been partially described in Section 2 above. These will now be looked at in further detail.

The characteristics associated with the currently active control may be found in the properties window. This is activated by the key *F4*, or by selecting the *Properties Window* from the *View* menu.

There are three main parts in the window. These are the control to which it refers, the properties of that control, and a description of the property which is currently selected. In the example shown in Figure 2.8, the component is a form whose name is *Form1*. This can be seen in the combo box at the top of the figure.

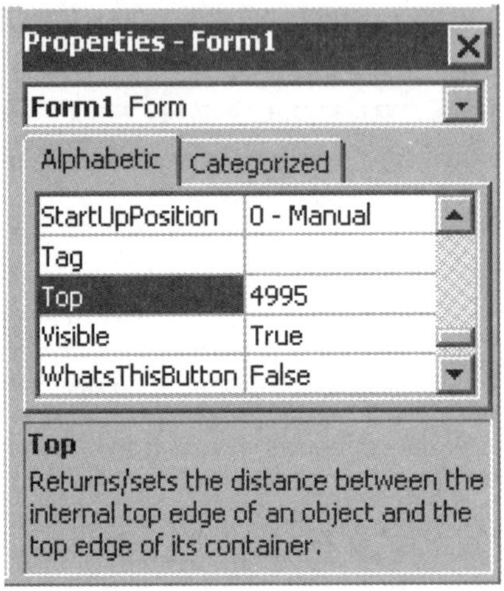

Figure 2.8 Control properties

The property selected in this example is *Top*. This defines where the top of the form appears when the program is running. This is shown in Figure 2.8 at position 4995, or about 9 centimetres from the top of the main window. More information about the selected property is shown in the bottom part of the window. The information in the example is a description of the *Top* property.

Some of the properties are set at the time that a Visual Program is designed and constructed, and cannot afterwards be altered – without, that is, modifying and recompiling the program. Other properties may be changed from within the program while it is running. *Top* is an example of the latter, in that it may be changed while a program is being executed.

———————— CRUCIAL CONCEPT ————————

All controls have **properties**, some of which can be set during the running of a program. Some, however, are fixed when the program is compiled, and cannot then be altered.

Another property, similar to *Top*, is *Left*. This specifies the position of the left-hand side of the form, and it can also be changed during the execution of the program. Two more properties which describe the position of the form are *Height* and *Width*, as mentioned in Section 2. Setting any of these in the properties window will change the corresponding appearance of the form. Similar changes will occur if their values are changed while the program is running. Their names are those of the corresponding variables.

In addition to changing the values of these properties, it is possible, during the execution of the program, to find their current values. This is also straightforward, and using their names as variables will return the current setting for these properties. An example of this is shown below; at the same time, a new event is described.

When a program starts, the form it is based on is made **active**. The method associated with this activation event is *Form_Activate*, and is called at this time. Any code included in this subroutine will be executed at this time. When the code shown below is executed, the initial position of the left-hand side of the form will be displayed.

```
Private Sub Form_Activate()
    ' Show where the left-hand side of the form is at this time
    Print "The left-hand side is at "; Left
End Sub
```

CRUCIAL ACTIVITY

Design your own code fragments and embed them in the subroutine code. Execute the resulting program.

When organising the properties of any control, it is sometimes easier to set up items with similar characteristics. By using the **Categorized** tab (see Figure 2.8), separate properties are grouped for ease of reference. The four properties mentioned above (*Top*, *Left*, *Height* and *Width*) all appear in the **Position** category.

It is also simple, when designing Visual Programs, to make approximate choices for some properties. These may be adjusted according to a user's preferences, and formalised at a later stage. An example of this is when adjusting the size of a form. It may be resized as a window, by a 'click and drag' mouse operation. The *Height* and *Width* properties may be seen to alter correspondingly as this takes place.

Quick test

1. How does Visual Basic assist with program layout prototyping?
2. Name four properties of a typical Visual Basic control.

Section 8

Further control details

In this section, you will learn more about selected controls.

Other controls have already been mentioned in Section 4 – option buttons, labels, text boxes and pictures. Two of these will be described in more detail. The organisation of controls held within a form will also be illustrated by examples. It is assumed that the instructions given below will be followed as they are described; and that suitable notes will also be taken.

The two controls to be described here are **labels** and **text boxes**. These are set up in a form, using the toolbox, and their exact size or positioning will not be important at this stage. When the program is running, the user will be able to change the text shown by the label – it will be organised to match whatever has been typed into the text box. This change will take place when the mouse is clicked on the form.

It is useful to distinguish carefully between these two controls. A label, as you might expect, is for adding a name to some part of the form. It is not intended that a user can change it during the running of a Visual Program. A text box, however, is intended to display text which may also be altered; although it may be for display purposes only.

Form_Click is the event which will cause this to take place, as in the example in Section 3. It will therefore be necessary to take the value of the text shown in the text box at this time, and assign it to the label being displayed. First, however, the label and text box controls should be positioned on the form.

There are now three controls within the Visual Program. They are easy to select, if any changes are to be made. At the top of the **Properties** window there is a combo box holding the available controls: selecting the control automatically allows its properties to be changed as required. Alternatively, a single click on the control selects its properties in the same way.

The code will be added to the *Form_Click* method; but the effects are not to take place within the form itself, but rather in the label and the text box. The source for the information is the contents of the text box: the **text** attribute is described as 'the text contained in the control', which is what is needed here. It is to be sent to the 'name' of the label: this is the **caption**, and its description is given similarly.

―――――――――――――――――――― CRUCIAL CONCEPT ――――――――――――――――――――
The method called when the mouse button is clicked inside a form is *Form_Click*.

The properties of each control show that a caption is a property common to all of them. Because of this, the use of the identifier `caption` on its own will not be sufficient to distinguish which of the three captions is to be used. It is therefore necessary to be able to identify the components of one control from within a different control. This is done using a full name of any property. This name is constructed by naming the control whose property is to be used, following this with a dot ('.'), and then adding the name of the property. (This will work in any component; so that a full name of this kind may also be used within a component when referring to itself.)

Thus the source to be used is *Text1.Text* (assuming that the default name of the text box is *Text1*). The destination, assuming a similar default name, is *Label1.Caption*. The instruction to be added to the *Form_Click* method is therefore

```
Label1.Caption = Text1.Text
```

There is no other event to be used in this program; this method will carry out all that is needed (see Figure 2.9).

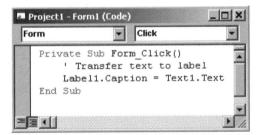

Figure 2.9 Example of method

―――――――――――――――――――― CRUCIAL ACTIVITY ――――――――――――――――――――
It is now appropriate to run the program. This is done as suggested in Section 3.

While the program is running, it is obvious that no change takes place in the label until the necessary event (click within the form) takes place. Changing the text in the text box is not enough. It is also easy to see that the *Form_Click* event cannot take place within the outlines of the label or the text box. An example of the appearance of the program, as it is being executed, is shown in Figure 2.10.

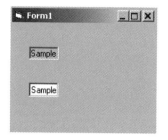

Figure 2.10 Event-driven example

The program may be closed down using any of the possibilities given at the end of Section 3.

Quick test

1. How is one control referred to from the code written for another control?

2. Name two control properties which may be changed during the execution of a Visual Program.

Section 9

Appearance of the program code

In this section, you will learn about customising the appearance of a Visual Program.

While you are working with Visual Basic, you can affect the way the code text appears on your screen. There is a default set up, shown in Figure 2.11. You find this from the *Tools* command on the *Options* menu, under *Editor Format*. You can change many of the settings, even in ways that are not useful. (It is **not** a good idea to have green text on a green background, for instance.) In most cases, it is worth leaving everything as it is.

Figure 2.11 Appearance editing

―――――――――― CRUCIAL ACTIVITY ――――――――――

As an example, however, change the *Keyword Text* to an alternative colour. Check the effect this has on the appearance of the code.

This may not appear to be particularly important. It is, however, one of the ways in which programs may be presented more effectively. If it is possible to improve the appearance of anything and make it easier to work with, this is an advantage. It introduces less strain, the users do not tire so rapidly, and consequently are less liable to make mistakes. It is one further aspect of the importance of good interface design and implementation. This, of course, applies also to the products of Visual Programming, as well as the environments in which they are developed.

Quick test

Why might it be good practice to change the colours or sizes of Visual Program code?

End of chapter assessment

Questions

1. What is a *Form_Click*, and what can it be used for?
2. How many twips are there in 2 centimetres?
3. Name three fundamental principles of good software engineering practice.
4. Which is better for viewing: blue letters on a white background, or yellow letters on a black background? (This should be tested by use of the *Editor Format* option.)
5. How many categories of control are there?
6. How is the Toolbox displayed?
7. How are controls selected and positioned on a form?
8. What are the keywords which start and end the code for a method?

Answers

1. *Form_Click* is a method within the code of a form which is entered when a mouse click event takes place while the mouse pointer is inside the form's borders. It can be used to hold the code to perform any action appropriate to the program's needs.
2. There are $2 \times 567 = 1134$ twips in 2 centimetres.
3. These include code reproducibility, stability, robustness, reuse, understandability – there are several other possibilities.
4. This is actually a matter of individual perception – the author prefers blue on white, but does not insist that is correct for you. However: did you notice the side-effects?
5. The Help system refers to three categories in Visual Basic 6.0: **Intrinsic controls**, such as the command button and frame controls; **ActiveX controls,** which exist as separate files with a .ocx file name extension; and **Insertable Objects**, such as a Microsoft Excel Worksheet. (This is not meant to introduce new ideas, but to illustrate the use of the Help facility.)
6. By selecting *Toolbox* from the *View* menu, or using the **Toolbox** button on the toolbar.
7. The control is selected from the toolbox and positioned on the form using 'drag and drop'. (This also allows the control's size to be specified.)
8. The method starts with 'Private Sub' and ends with 'End Sub'.

Further reading and research

http://web.nps.navy.mil/~gazolla/is3001/files/VBintro.ppt holds an interesting introduction to many aspects of event-driven programs centred around Visual Basic.
Kipling, R. (1908). *Just So Stories*, MacMillan & Co. Ltd.

Chapter 3
Constructing a
small application

Chapter summary

This chapter deals with the development of a Visual Programming application. It uses a number of the controls and forms the basis of development of event-driven programming for the remainder of the book.

Learning outcomes

This chapter introduces the learning outcomes to enable the professional approach to producing a Visual Program. When you have successfully completed this chapter, you will be able to:

Outcome 1: Design a Visual Program in a professional way.

Outcome 2: Implement a Visual Program and its code according to a specified design.

Outcome 3: Place controls in a form to construct an efficient and consistent interface.

Outcome 4: Test a Visual Program to ensure that it conforms to its specification.

Outcome 5: Identify areas for future program development.

How will you be assessed on this?

Typically you may be asked to produce a simple Visual Program involving file reading and writing. You may also be asked to answer questions about a simple program lifecycle, about specific controls, chosen program methods and the uses of certain operators.

Section 1

Building the foundations

In this section, you will be reminded about approaches to correct program construction.

When constructing a house which is to be satisfactory and safe to live in, the first thing to do is to draw up a set of plans for the builders to follow. With these, a prospective buyer could be reasonably certain that the house would have the right number of rooms, connecting with each other in a reasonable way, and able to hold furniture and fittings so as to make the house into a home. Without such plans, the results would be unpredictable, and there would be no way of knowing whether the house would be what was wanted at all.

Once the plans were decided on and agreed, the building could go ahead. It would be constructed in an agreed order – it is fair to assume that the roof would not be the earliest item to be built. First would come the foundations, and other parts would be built on to these. Some parts might be constructed separately, and added into their correct places when it was time to do so. When the whole was complete, the buyer and the architect would check that the builder had carried out the agreed plan. The house would be fit for its purpose – that of being lived in.

The same approach works with other constructions, such as cars and aeroplanes. It should not therefore be a surprise that computer programs behave in the same way. They should be planned, constructed according to an agreed scheme and tested to make sure that they behave in the way in which the user intended. The detailed requirements are not the same as for a car, because the tasks which a program is expected to carry out are not the same as those which a car is expected to carry out. But the same approach should be used: that of agreed design, orderly construction and careful testing.

It will also be appropriate to maintain a set of plans of the construction. As a householder who has had some building work done, your author has found the importance of knowing where previous plumbing and wiring had taken place when some changes were needed. The builders' plans helped very much in this situation, and it was a straightforward matter to change and extend the existing facilities using the existing drawings.

In the same way, it is important for any programmer to provide working plans for anyone who may wish to change the existing programs. Because of the complexity of such plans, there may also be a need to provide a simplified set for those users who need to know what the program is intended to do. These would not involve all of the technical details needed by a maintenance programmer, but would hold information about interfaces which the user was expected to employ.

CRUCIAL TIP

The right time to produce documentation is before the work is done. It can be changed if necessary; and it is simpler to change something which already exists than to make it up as a new item.

The work to be carried out in this chapter will follow that path. The requirements for a small program will be developed in two parts: those in which the user will be interested and those with which the programmer will be more concerned. Naturally, the programmer will need to know about all of the work to be done, but it will be obvious that the user will be less interested in what is going on 'behind the walls' – not of the house, of course, but of the program. Some aspects will therefore be plain to the user, but anything which is not necessary will be hidden away.

CRUCIAL CONCEPT

The idea of **information hiding** is important – anything which is not essential to an activity may be safely hidden away so as not to interfere with the processes being considered.

Quick test

1. Why is information hiding an important aspect of program development?

2. What kinds of documentation are essential to every computer program?

Section 2

Event-driven systems

You will be introduced to some design approaches for Visual Programs.

Visual Programs are, of course, like many other kinds of computer programs. They are intended to solve a problem which a user may encounter, and in doing so to save work. But there are some aspects where they differ from programs which may be left running under their own control. They will typically provide an interface for the user to control and to change the course of the program's execution. These two aspects of Visual Programs are separate, and it is important that each of them is understood.

The visual interface between the user and the program must be constructed to give and receive information in a carefully controlled way. Because much of the material will be essentially pictorial, even though it consists of words and other text, this must be taken into account. For instance, as was mentioned in Chapter 2, the colours used in a Visual Program are important. It is not sufficient merely to display text for a user to see, but it must be done in a way which will not cause difficulty in reading. Text must also be of a reasonable size, and laid out in an efficient way to enable communication readily. As the same applies to printed information, this should not be an unfamiliar aspect of design to a programmer.

The ways in which the program is executed, however, may not be so familiar. It is not sufficient to decide what a program will do once the inputs from a file have been presented to it. All of the control possibilities which a human user may choose **while the program is running** must also be taken into account. These decisions will be signalled to the Visual Program as a series of **events** which will have to be foreseen. The appropriate action may then be taken in each case.

CRUCIAL CONCEPT

Event-driven systems have particular characteristics which must be taken into account during program design.

In this chapter, these points will be taken into account. However, many of the possible events will be ignored. As an example of this simplification (see Chapter 7 for some further aspects of this approach), the only mouse-based events taken into account will be single clicks. Perhaps surprisingly, in the light of the example to be implemented (see Section 3), no keyboard-based events will be acknowledged.

From these statements, it should be understood that one of the aspects of design for event-driven systems is the need for a list (or similar record) of those events which are to be used. It will not necessarily be complete in the first draft of the design, but should be fully incorporated before implementation is started. It will typically include mouse-click events for button controls, change events for sliders, and similar items.

There is one other aspect of which you should be aware when considering program events. These events do not always come from user intervention. There may also be events generated by the execution of the Visual Program itself, or by the operating system. Examples of these include errors and timing events. The former are probably already familiar, and include attempting to read past the end of a file, or attempting to divide by zero. Timing events may be set up with a specific purpose so that a user has a certain time to make a response, after which pre-decided alternative actions are undertaken by default.

Quick test

1. What are important attributes of text in a Visual Program?

2. How do event-driven programs differ from other procedural programs?

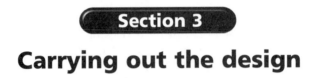

Carrying out the design

You will learn the approaches needed to design a Visual Program and its interface.

The application which will be used to show the construction of a Visual Program will be based on a simple text display program. It will be designed by reference to the controls used for the program. These will be placed in the correct places on the form, and the associated code will be defined. The system will be tested to show that it is ready for its users.

The user's interface with the Visual Program is shown in Figure 3.1. It is based on a single form control, which holds two text box controls, six button controls and three label controls. Files may be loaded or saved using the buttons in the top right-hand corner of the form (*Load*, *Save* and *Cancel*). For display purposes, the text may be shown in one of three possible sizes, here named *Large*, *Medium* and *Small*. The file name of the text file will be given in the upper text box (*File*), while the text contained in the file will be shown in the larger text box below it (*Editor*). This text display application will have very few of the facilities normally associated with such programs. Some aspects, however, will be included as defaults.

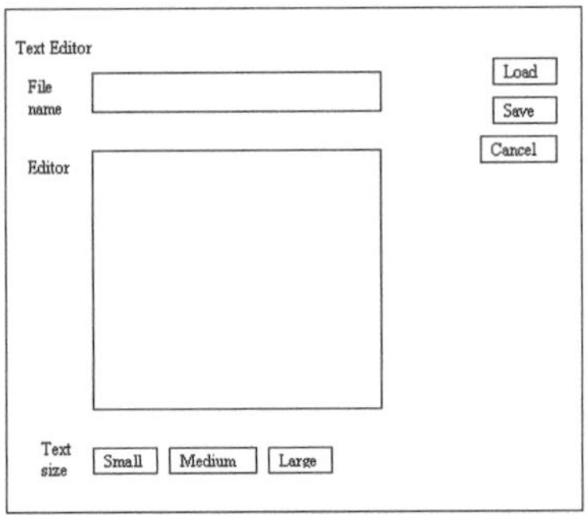

Figure 3.1 Text display program design

Many of the attributes of the controls might theoretically be left with their default values. However, it is usually better to replace the default name and caption with descriptions more appropriate to the application being constructed. The names and functions of each control, whether in its external form for the user or its internal form for the programmer, are best chosen with a mnemonic significance. In that way, it is less likely that mistakes will be made during either the use or the implementation of the program.

To help with debugging, the names will describe both the functions of the controls and their types. These are tabulated in Figure 3.2. (The approach to naming used here is known as **Hungarian Notation**. It is dealt with at greater length in Chapter 6.) This is distinct from the word identifying each control while the Visual Program is being executed, which is known as its **caption**.

Control	Name	Caption
Form	frmEditor	*Text Editor*
Text box	txtFile	
Text box	txtEditor	
Button	cmdLoad	*Load*
Button	cmdSave	*Save*
Button	cmdCancel	*Cancel*
Button	cmdSmall	*Small*
Button	cmdMedium	*Medium*
Button	cmdLarge	*Large*
Label	lblFile	*File*
Label	lblEditor	*Editor*
Label	lblTextSize	*Text Size*

Figure 3.2 Control attributes

CRUCIAL CONCEPT

It is important for different aspects of a Visual Program to be kept consistent: this leads to fewer chances to make mistakes.

Comparison between Figures 3.1 and 3.2 shows the use of the caption. The name of each control has no effect on the external appearance of the Visual Program, only appearing in the program code. It is the equivalent of an identifier used for naming variables in other computer languages. The prefix cmd used for each button is a reminder that the control is more formally called a **Command Button**.

There are two more attributes which have to be taken into account in the design of this Visual Program. These concern the text box controls. As each will be allowed to vary, they must not be *lock*ed; and because the *Editor* window will contain multiple lines, this must be allowed in its properties.

CRUCIAL ACTIVITY

Place examples of a Command Button, a Text Box and a Label on a Form. Look at the properties of each control. Identify the items described in this section so far. Make suitable notes.

The appearance of the Visual Program is the next aspect to consider. This can be drawn roughly on paper, and then used to design the appearance of the application. A suggestion for this layout has been shown in Figure 3.1; but this may not be the final one chosen. However, some particular points should be noted about the placing of the controls, and their sizes.

The command buttons have been grouped into two sets, according to their function. They are all the same size, and they are arranged in a rectangular array. The same typeface and size have been used for all of the captions on the form, which is the default. The text boxes have the same width, but the filename box has only the height for a single line of text. All of these points should be checked using the properties of each control.

CRUCIAL TIP

Always adopt a consistent approach to layout; and check it carefully.

All of the activities described to this point are fixed aspects of the Visual Program. These aspects are implemented using the **design view** of the project. This view also enables the program code to be added to the project. Some control properties can also be modified while the Visual Program is running; others, including the program code, cannot be changed at this time.

The remaining part of the design should be familiar from previous experience. As this will be using new programming aspects, there will be language specific items with which to become acquainted, but these are not complex. Because the only activities taking place are associated with the command buttons, these are the only explicit coding aspects to be dealt with. Each will require its own design activity according to the associated purpose.

The size of the characters displayed is an attribute of the *Editor* text box: this is one of the properties that can be altered during the running of the program. This will be dealt with by the three command buttons called cmdSmall, cmdMedium and cmdLarge. A typical approach to the design for these buttons is given for cmdMedium as pseudocode:

cmdMedium: Change text box text size to 10 points.

This is sufficient to define the activity to take place when the click event is detected by the system event manager. The other two corresponding buttons have similar designs associated with them.

The remaining design aspects to be attended to are associated with the other command buttons: cmdLoad, cmdSave and cmdCancel. The first of these will load a file from the backing store into the *Editor* text box, the second will store the contents of the text box into the designed file and terminate the program. The third command button will simply terminate the program. The design for that event may be described as:

cmdCancel: Terminate the Visual Program.

─────── CRUCIAL ACTIVITY ───────

Complete the pseudocode design for the remaining command buttons.

Quick test

1. With which controls are events typically associated?
2. Name some attributes of controls on a form to be treated consistently for best results.

Section 4

Placing the controls

In this section you will learn some of the details of consistent design presentation.

It is now time to move into the first part of converting the design into the corresponding implementation. The rough sketch shown in Figure 3.1 is good enough to give an idea about what is expected. It will not be good enough, though, to present to a user, even though it has enough detail to demonstrate the functionality of the design.

The controls are selected one at a time from the toolbar. They are placed in the area where they will be needed and their sizes are adjusted. As the size changes, its width and height are displayed. Corresponding controls, for example the command buttons, should be given their appropriate sizes using these figures as guidance.

You will see, as you carry these changes out, that the sizes do not change smoothly, but in fixed increments according to a pattern of dots on the form. These dots form a uniform grid, and it is common for the controls being positioned with their sides placed according to these grid points. It is recommended that advantage is taken of this facility, because it allows the simple alignment of all controls. (If this does not appear to be happening, make sure that the *Align controls to grid* box is checked in the *General* part of the *Options* menu under *Tools*.)

The alignment should also allow for the equal spacing of similar controls. In Figure 3.3, each button in the two groups is spaced uniformly within its group. The labels shown are aligned in a column, and placed similarly with respect to the controls they describe.

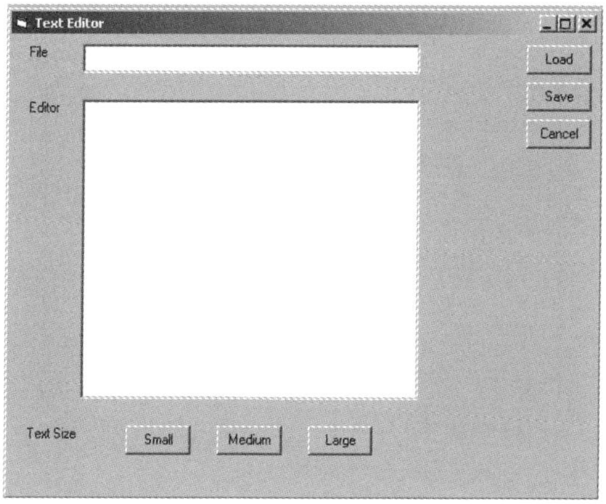

Figure 3.3 Text display program interface

It is at this time that the controls should be given their names and their captions. This may be carried out easily, following the use of a table similar to that shown in Figure 3.2. The properties menu associated with each control in turn may be accessed by double-clicking the control, or by the methods described in Chapter 2. The user's view of the form will then be defined in a consistent fashion.

──────── CRUCIAL TIP ────────

Use the design view in conjunction with previous design work, and make sure that all of the naming changes have been carried out before any coding starts.

The final work to be carried out at this stage will ensure that the text boxes can be changed if necessary, and that the large text box will be able to hold more than a single line of text. The properties corresponding to this are, respectively, *Locked* and *Multiline*. *Locked* should be set to *False* in both cases; and *Multiline* set *True* for the large text box.

Quick test

1. In what way does the layout grid help in Visual Programming?

2. What is the best order for adjusting names and positions of controls in a Visual Program? Why is this?

Section 5

Program coding for the controls

In this section you will learn about typical code sequences used in Visual Programs.

All of the work done so far has produced code for the Visual Program. It might not be obvious what that code should contain. It can be checked by saving the work done so far, and looking at the text view of the file defining the Form. This shows the sizing and positions of the controls, their names and any other aspects of their formatting.

It is now appropriate to add the active code. There will be a single subroutine for each command button, which will be activated by the *Click* event associated with that button. A typical example of this is shown in Figure 3.4. The first and last lines will already have been made available by the Visual Basic system. It has been informed that a command button has been named cmdMedium, and has prepared a typical event for that button called cmdMedium_Click.

```
Private Sub cmdMedium_Click()
'
'    Set text size to 10 points
'

        txtEditor.Font.Size = 10

End Sub
```

Figure 3.4 Change font size subroutine

Lines 2-4 form a typical commentary heading for the subroutine. Such heading should always be included, as a valuable part of the internal documentation process. The only active line in the subroutine follows, setting the *Size* of the Font of the large text box, txtEditor, to 10. The dot notation has been previously mentioned in Chapter 2, and this is a typical use of that notation. You will see, when the program is executed, that this applies to all of the text showing in the box. No more need be done to alter that size.

─── CRUCIAL ACTIVITY ───

Write the (similar) subroutines for the other two *Size* buttons.

The contents of the cmdCancel subroutine are minimal, but necessary. All that is required is to close the Visual Program and return to the operating system. This may be done by the single method End.

The other two subroutines are associated with cmdLoad and cmdSave. It is important to understand the way in which reading and writing of strings is carried out to implement these. In each case, the file to be used should be opened, the input or output carried out, and the file is then closed. In the case of cmdSave, the Visual Program may then be closed by using End, in the same way as cmdCancel.

The Open statement has the form

$$Open \quad PathName \quad For \quad Mode \quad As \quad \#FileNumber$$

where *PathName* is a string holding the name of the file to be opened, *PathName* is either Input or Output, and *FileNumber* is an integer by which the file will be referred to during future processing. As the file will be opened, processed and closed within each subroutine, and no other files are used, *FileNumber* may be simply set to 1 in each case.

The detailed coding used to save the file is shown in Figure 3.5. It is sufficient to open the file for output using the file name given in the smaller text box, write the contents of the larger text box to the file, and close it. The Visual Program system takes care of all other activities. The buffer associated with the text box is defined using the name of the text box, and specifying the Text item using dot notation.

```
Private Sub cmdSave_Click()
'
' Write file and close
'
    Open txtFile.Text For Output As #1
    Print #1, txtEditor.Text
    Close #1
    End
End Sub
```

Figure 3.5 Write subroutine

For input, the situation is slightly more complex. During the standard reading of a text input file, it is assumed that it consists of a set of single-line strings, terminated by suitable separators. These have therefore to be processed to make a structure appropriate for the text box which is to hold them. This is done by concatenating them, while separating them with a newline – here formed from the characters whose character values are 13 and 10 respectively.

Two independent variables will be required here: one to hold the newline construction, and one to hold each line of text as it is read in. These are declared using the Dim statement in the format shown in Figure 3.6 (the s-prefix reminds the programmer that the variables are strings). The variable sCRLF is formed by concatenating the two characters using the & operator. (A similar construction will be encountered again in Chapter 7.)

```
Private Sub cmdLoad_Click()
Dim sInputLine, sCRLF As String
'
' Read file
'
    sCRLF = Chr(13) & Chr(10)
    Open txtFile.Text For Input As #1
    Do While Not EOF(1)
        Input #1, sInputLine
        txtEditor.Text = _
            txtEditor.Text & _
            sInputLine & sCRLF
    Loop
    Close #1
End Sub
```

Figure 3.6 Read subroutine

The file is opened, and its contents are read until the end of file is reached: it is then closed and the subroutine is exited. Within the reading loop, the lines are read successively, and concatenated into the text buffer of the text box txtFile.

CRUCIAL ACTIVITY

Look up the Open, Input and Print statements using the Help files. Take appropriate notes.

As described in Chapter 2, these methods show how some of the properties of a control may be altered during the running of a Visual Program, as well as at its design stage. In some cases, these properties may be used to give useful values for further activities. txtEditor.Text, as shown in Figure 3.6, is an example of both of these uses.

CRUCIAL CONCEPT

Control properties are set at design time. It is sometimes correct to amend control properties while a program is running. You need to be aware of when each approach is appropriate when a Visual Program is being designed.

Two lines of the code in Figure 3.6 end with the underscore character '_'. This is a continuation character. It allows long lines of text to be contained in a window, to help with layout and comprehension. In Figure 3.6, the effect is to allow the concatenation statement to be written on three lines, but to be considered as a single unit of execution.

Quick test

1. What suffix is used for a typical command button event?
2. What is the importance of the Dim statement?

Section 6

System testing

You will be reminded of ways in which a Visual Program should be tested.

The next stage after implementation is testing. The paths through the Visual Program will be inspected, and suitable test data constructed to verify that all works as expected. This should not show any unexpected outcomes in a simple program, but it is still important to be able to show that the implementation is what was expected. In the following section, it is assumed that nothing has gone wrong. That is something to aim for, but if there are any errors, there is no cause to worry. Identifying them and then correcting them is not a complex operation.

CRUCIAL TIP

Make sure you have saved your work before going any further.

The first approach should be to make sure that the Visual Program works on simple data. For this purpose, you will need to construct a simple text file with a few lines in it, none of them too long. Save it in a file with a simple name – you will need to type this name to find it again. (If all is working well, there is a simple way to do this … see below.)

There are six simple commands to check, each with an independent subroutine. However, three of them, for changing the text size, are similar, and can be verified in one test run.

These will be checked first. Therefore, start the program as described in Chapter 2. Position the cursor in the large text box and type some characters.

Now click on the sizing buttons in turn, and watch the changes that take place. If everything is in order, the size should change in the expected manner. You can then test the *Cancel* button, which should stop the program and return to the Visual Basic environment.

This has involved four working lines of program code, one in each subroutine. If anything has not gone according to expectations, it should be corrected straight away. But first, how should it be identified? Taking the *Cancel* button activity, there are two things to check: is the *End* method correct – has it been spelt properly? (The seemingly simple mistakes are the hardest to correct: we see what we **want** to see, not always what is necessarily present.) And – is there an attempt to execute it (in other words, was the subroutine entered)? Check that the spelling of the subroutine name has not been altered by mistake. If the name of the command button (plus _Click) does not correspond to the name of the subroutine, when the button is 'pressed', nothing will happen. And there will be no warning!

CRUCIAL CONCEPT

Not every error is signalled actively. Sometimes 'nothing happening' is as much warning as there is.

The programmer has received considerable help by this time, without asking for it. The cursor, denoting the working text box, is supplied automatically. To position that cursor, the mouse and the arrow keys do not have to be given special instructions. To add text, or to delete text, no special 'extras' are called for. This additional help will often be there without being requested; but it is always safer to check.

CRUCIAL ACTIVITY

Try to discover if there are any other 'standard' facilities available without asking.

That leaves two subroutines to be tested. The *Save* subroutine has simpler coding, and should be checked first. But it is first important to make a note of the text which was to be saved, and the filename of the file used, as you will wish to check that both of these have been used correctly. It is also very dangerous indeed, because there is no checking performed here at all. If you accidentally specified a system file name, it would be replaced by your new file. If you are satisfied that damage is unlikely, go ahead. But be careful. Start the program, type some text, type a filename in the small text box, and click on *Save*.

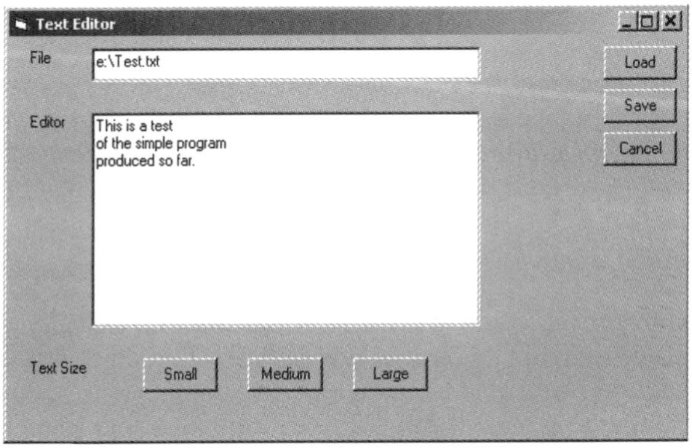

Figure 3.7 Testing the program

Now retrieve the file you have just produced using a text viewer (Windows 2000 provides 'Notepad' for this). Check that its contents are as they should be. If so, you now have a simple program for preparing short text files.

CRUCIAL TIP

Give the full pathname of the file. That makes it easier to find.

Now test the Load subroutine against the specification. You already have a named file, because you have just produced it. Start the program, type the filename in the small text box, and click on Load. This should retrieve the file. But this is also an opportunity to find out what happens if there is a fault. If you specify a file that does not exist, and try to retrieve it, the system points out your error to you. It is important to try this, because it is part of any reasonable testing sequence.

There are some particular items to be aware of at this point. Look at the 'standard' editor facilities of copying, cutting and pasting text. These may not appear in the original specification. However, the functionality provided by the Visual Basic system has many such standard features which are built in. Another of these is an 'undo' feature. If these do not appear in the specification, should they be tested? The safest way to approach this is to look at the system from the point of view of a user. If the facilities provided are useful, they should be included in the specification, even if it means rewriting it. They will then be included in the testing activity in the customary way. If they are not useful, or possibly even harmful, they should be removed if that is possible. If it is not possible, due warning should be included in the documentation.

Quick test

1. Which errors are the most dangerous?

2. In what order should testing take place?

Section 7

Extending the implementation

You will learn about some of the shortcomings of the example, and how they might be dealt with.

It is important to be aware that this is a simple and incomplete example. There are several aspects which prevent this being a fully operational program. Some would be reasonably straightforward to amend; others would require more effort.

It has already been suggested that the program is unsafe in its file handling. If a file is requested to be read, but does not exist, a system message is generated. This has the information, but not in a friendly form. Further, there is no way of recovering in a controlled fashion after an error has been dealt with in this manner. It is often preferable to allow user interaction if an error occurs in an interactive program, with a view to attempting to correct the situation causing the fault.

Another shortcoming of the example program arises from no warning being given if the program is about to overwrite an already existing file. This is not difficult to organise in theory, but depends on being able to cause an error on purpose. The file to be written is first opened as if it is to be read. If this succeeds, the file is immediately closed and the warning is given that the file already exists: it will only be overwritten if that is acceptable to the user. If the attempt to open generates an error, because the file does not exist, then it is safe to write without further problem.

There are other aspects which might be useful if the specification were extended. Perhaps it would be useful to copy, cut and paste text; but these facilities are not part of the specification. It might be desirable to offer alternative ways of specifying the drive and folder in which a file exists, but again this has not been specified in advance. Each of these alterations is not complex in itself, but it would need more work to incorporate such extensions.

> ──── CRUCIAL TIP ────
>
> More haste, less speed.

In any case, there is a sensible way to carry out such alterations, and an alternative which is not so sensible. Even though it appears very tempting to add a small item to a Visual Program of this nature, it is far better to return to the beginning of the design, implementation and testing cycle and to start afresh. It will lead to less work in the long run, and will develop a more stable product. This example will be revisited in Chapter 6, to organise part of the visual interface in a safer way.

> ──── CRUCIAL CONCEPT ────
>
> There is no such thing as a **small** change.

There is a final stage which has been deferred for the time being. A Visual Program should be packaged as a whole unit before being distributed to its users. This will be dealt with in Chapter 10.

Quick test

1. What is the safest way of altering a Visual Program?

2. Why would you want to read from a file which is to be written to?

Section 8

End of chapter assessment

Questions

1. What stages does a Visual Program pass through between the initial idea and the final product? What is the common thread connecting the whole?
2. Name six kinds of event that are associated with a text box.
3. What are two typical attributes associated with Forms, Text boxes, Command buttons and Labels?
4. What method is used to terminate the execution of a Visual Program?
5. Why should a programmer be careful when altering a Visual Program?
6. Name three mandatory parameters for the Open method.
7. What is the & operator used for?
8. Which menu is used to describe and alter the appearance of a Visual Basic control?

Answers

1. Specification and refinement; design; coding/implementation; testing; packaging and distribution. All of these stages should be accompanied by relevant documentation.
2. These include *Change, Click, GotFocus, KeyDown, KeyUp, LostFocus, MouseDown, MouseUp* and *Validate*. There are many more of these.
3. Each of these controls typically has a Name and a Caption.
4. A Visual Program is terminated by the method End.
5. Because there is no such thing as a **small** change.

6. Each Open method must specify a filename, a mode of transfer (for example, input or output) and a file number.

7. The & operator is used to join two strings together (concatenate them).

8. The properties menu describes each Visual Basic control, and allows its design-time properties to be defined.

Section 9

Further reading and research

Brooks, Frederick P. Jr. (1979). *The Mythical Man-Month: Essays on Software Engineering*, Addison-Wesley. ISBN 0–201–00650–2.

http://www.knowledgehound.com/topics/vb.htm has a wide range of topics to follow up, including approaches to testing.

Chapter 4
Use of a Development Environment

Chapter summary

This chapter is designed to tell you what a Development Environment is, why it is important and how to get the best out of it.

Learning outcomes

The outcomes of this chapter are related to efficient development of a Visual Program. When you have completed the chapter successfully, you will be able to:

Outcome 1: Discuss the functions of a Development Environment.

Outcome 2: Use a Development Environment to assist in producing error-free programs.

Outcome 3: Step through program instruction code for debugging purposes.

Outcome 4: Inspect and if necessary change the values of program variables during debugging.

How will you be assessed on this?

Using a new or existing Visual Program, you may be asked to display and change the values of variables and how the paths through a Visual Program may be traced in an interactive session. You may also have to answer questions about the use of a Development Environment.

Section 1

What is a Development Environment?

You will find out more about the Visual Basic Development Environment.

You have already been briefly introduced, in Chapter 1, to the Development Environment which applies to this kind of Visual Programming. This will be built on in this chapter, although further aspects will be introduced at later stages of the book as they become applicable.

The Development Environment is, as its name states, an Environment. It is the context in which a program may execute whilst being developed. It is used during the development of a program. There are Development Environments for different languages and computer systems, each one configured for an appropriate combination of the two. A good Development Environment aims to be unobtrusive; but it will come rapidly to a programmer's assistance when it is needed.

Its task is to assist a programmer in the production of the code of an application, and to continue with that assistance while the application is being tested. For this reason, it typically includes a source editor and debugger. Further, it contains routines which correspond to typical testing strategies and routines which supply information about a program while it is being tested.

It is not necessary to use a Development Environment when constructing and executing programs. In fact, early computer programmers had no such assistance. There is, therefore, no compulsion to use such a tool. But, as with many other such labour-saving devices, it will make your life much easier if you do. The lack of it certainly made the lives of those early programmers much more difficult!

CRUCIAL CONCEPT

A Development Environment is not essential – but it is very useful indeed.

The next point to be made is that, to get the best out of a Development Environment, you need to be aware of what it can do for you. You also need to know how best to make use of its facilities. And you need to know what it cannot do. (The last part is simpler, as far as this book is concerned – but wait until you deal with VB Scripts and other language extensions in Chapter 7.)

Much of your active use of the Development Environment will appear to be with the debugger: especially when persuading a program to do what it was designed to do. Appearances are not always true, however. Whenever you add a Visual Control, or modify its properties, you are doing so with the assistance of the Development Environment. Whenever you create or modify source text, you are probably doing so with its help. It is, as it says, an Environment.

Quick test

1. What are the two major components of the Visual Basic Development Environment?
2. When is a Development Environment used?

Why is a Development Environment important?

This section gives the context and rationale for the use of a Development Environment.

Most importantly, the Development Environment is a strong support for the production of programs without errors. It cannot guarantee error-free production, but it can help in (at least) three ways:

- One way is in warning the programmer that an error has been made – this may be a simple spelling mistake, or a mistake in grammar (otherwise known as a 'syntax error'). As this will typically be discovered at an early stage of a program's input into the computer system, its effects can be minimised before they have a chance to spread and cause damage elsewhere in the program. An example of this is given in Figure 4.1: a variable has been used without being defined. This check is activated by the inclusion of the Option Explicit statement, and the Development Environment has been set to notify the programmer if this mistake has been made. This statement is placed outside the subroutine, typically at the head of the program code, as shown in Figure 4.1.

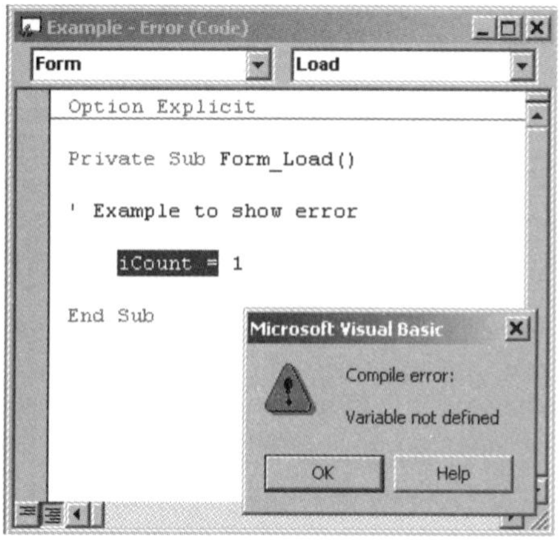

Figure 4.1 Error warning

CRUCIAL TIP

Always be ready to use the help that the Development Environment can give you.

- Another way is in assisting with a structured layout of the program text. This can be overridden, but it would be unwise to do so. The Development Environment points out different constructions, allowing the programmer more readily to recognise the structures being assembled. If these are not those which were intended, that fact is rapidly discovered.

- Yet another way is during a program's testing – this may be carried out systematically within the Development Environment, with easy access to the values of variables and the flow of control. The Development Environment will guard against catastrophes before they are allowed to cause trouble, and report them in an understandable way to the program developer.

What a Development Environment cannot do, however, is to guard against design or logical errors – where the program specification has not been followed, or where problems may arise at a later stage (when the program's execution may lead to unforeseen errors). There is still a place for the human developer which cannot be supplanted.

Quick test

1. Why is the layout of program code important?

2. What kind of errors can a Development Environment deal with directly?

Section 3

How to get the best out of a Development Environment

You will learn the most effective ways of using the Development Environment.

As with any other aspect of life, to get the best out of a Development Environment you must be aware of what it can – and cannot – offer you. For this reason, you will need to make yourself aware of the facilities offered by the Development Environment. This book will allow you to start the development of that awareness. But it cannot do the entire job on its own.

There are two other components which are available to you, both of which you should use. One is the Help facility included in the Visual Basic system – it contains the information relevant to the particular Development Environment used. (You will remember that this was introduced in Chapter 2.) The other is the practice which you must undertake yourself. The best way to discover the facilities of a system such as this is to try them out for yourself.

You must make notes while you do this: this will help you to remember what you have done, and when you did it. This will assist in fixing in your mind the activities associated with the use of the Development Environment. It will also make you more practised in recognising what the Development Environment can do in particular circumstances.

CRUCIAL TIP

You learn better when you write things down. You learn better still when you practise what you are learning. You learn best of all when you do both.

But there is nothing quite as important as having a well-thought-out plan **before** starting program development. The best time to work out what a Development Environment can do for you is when you are designing a program. At each stage of the conversion of a design into the corresponding code, you should ask yourself a number of questions (and make note of them and of the answers!). Among these are:

- which circumstances can arise during the execution of the program;
- which pathways are liable to be followed under those circumstances;
- what values of the variables are expected;
- what effect those values will have on the paths taken.

This will allow a testing plan to be drawn up, to be followed within the Development Environment. If the program generates an error during its execution, it will also allow the actual values of variables to be compared with their expected values, to find out whether these are significant in causing the error.

Fortunately, much of this work can be automated within the Development Environment. This will slow the execution down as you give the Development Environment more work to undertake, but that is unimportant when compared with the value of an error-free program.

But the Development Environment must be abandoned when the construction and testing program have been completed. It is not appropriate for the Development Environment to continue to be used for a working program for at least two reasons:

- The Development Environment would occupy storage which might otherwise be used by the production program if its use continued after the program had been completed. Within modern computer systems, with considerable storage capacity, this may not necessarily appear to be a serious matter. However, for packaging and providing an application to an end user, there are legal implications. The Development Environment as supplied with Visual Basic is subject to laws of copyright, and may not be supplied to others who have not purchased the usage rights.
- The Development Environment takes time to perform its activities, which may slow the execution of an application. Again, with modern computer systems, this may not appear to be of great importance. There are times, however, when slower responses to users' input may cause difficulties. For this reason also, the Development Environment should be discarded when its task has been (successfully) completed.

Quick test

1. When is it incorrect to use the Development Environment?

2. How can you find useful program development information?

Debugging tools in the Development Environment

You will gain an overview of the assistance available for debugging a Visual Program.

The debugging tools available in the Development Environment may typically be used in one of three ways. They may be called from the Visual Basic menu bar, from the Debug toolbar, or by suitable keystrokes. The menu bar is a little slower to use, but always present. Using keystrokes for debugging can be quicker, but is also more liable to lead to errors until the user becomes practised in their use. If you expect to be doing quite a lot of debugging, and want to be certain about what is happening, it is probably better to use the toolbar. If this is not visible, it should be called up from the *Toolbars* option on the *View* menu. It may appear on one, two or three lines, but the tools available are the same.

A three-line view of the Debugging Toolbar is given in Figure 4.2. The icons on the top line show straightforward execution: *Start, Pause* and *Stop*. The second line deals with stepping through the program code: setting or removing a breakpoint, and stepping into, over, or out of a routine. The three icons on the left of the bottom line are for windows to display the local variables, to carry out immediate calculations and to display variables that are being checked during execution; the right-hand two are for monitoring individual variables and to show the routines which are currently active.

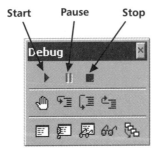

Figure 4.2 Debug toolbar: Start, Pause, Stop

That is quite a lot to consider at one time. In fact, not all of them will be dealt with in this book. Those being described will be introduced in a reasonable order, with specific examples to relate to each one.

The first three correspond most closely to normal program execution. The Visual Program may be started using the *Start* icon, and stopped using either of the *Pause* or the *Stop* icons. If you use the *Pause* icon, you can carry on again from where you stopped the program. If you use the *Stop* icon, the program has to be started again from the beginning.

─────── CRUCIAL ACTIVITY ───────

Load the program developed in Chapter 3. Start it using the Debug Toolbar. Stop it using the *Pause* icon. Restart it using the *Start* icon. Now use the *Stop* icon to stop it. Make a careful note of the difference in outcomes.

Quick test

1. What types of debugging assistance are available for program execution?

2. What types of debugging assistance are available for program variable values?

Section 5

Execution by stepping and using breakpoints

You will learn how to step through the code of a Visual Program.

It is sometimes useful, if it has become particularly difficult to discover the reason for an error, to execute a program one instruction at a time. As this can become extremely time-consuming, it should not be done as a matter of course. Work of this kind should be carefully planned before the debugging starts, so as to avoid inserting new errors where none existed before. But, when there is no other way forward, it is good to be ready to use the tools provided for just such an emergency.

CRUCIAL TIP

More haste, less speed. Planning ahead saves trouble later.

To execute the Visual Program one statement at a time, the *Step Into* tool is used (see Figure 4.3). This starts the program at the present position and carries out the work of exactly one statement. Program execution is then set to continue at the beginning of the next statement. This is particularly significant if the statement executed is a call to a function or a procedure (this will be referred to as 'procedure' in the remainder of this chapter). In this case, the next statement is the first one in that procedure.

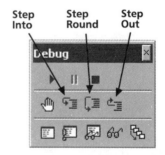

Figure 4.3 Debug toolbar: Step Into, Step Round, Step Out

If this level of detail is not needed – for example, the procedure may already have been successfully verified as correct – the *Step Round* tool may be used. If it is a simple statement, the step which takes place is the same as that for the *Step Into* tool. If the current statement is a procedure, it is executed in its entirety, and the statement after it is next to be obeyed. This provides a more rapid way of stepping through a program, but should only be used if the parts being stepped over are trustworthy.

The *Step Out* tool is used where a sequence of statements is being tested inside a procedure. If you are satisfied with the testing carried out at this point, and the remainder of the statements of the procedure have already been tested, the *Step Out* tool will execute the rest of the instructions. The next statement to be executed is the first statement after the procedure call.

CRUCIAL ACTIVITY

Set a Visual Program ready for execution, and use the *Step Into, Step Round* and *Step Out* tools to become familiar with their effects.

This approach, whilst extremely controlled in its effects, may lead to a considerable amount of unnecessary work. However, when debugging a Visual Program, attention is often concentrated on a very small number of statements in a known location. The remainder of the program is assumed to be correct.

CRUCIAL TIP

When using this approach, be certain that the above situation is true. Executing parts of a program in an unproved state leads to uncertain situations.

It is easier, more convenient and safer to suspend execution of the program immediately before the statements to be checked, and then step through them. This is carried out using the *Breakpoint* approach.

When a program is being tested with breakpoints set on one or more of its statements, execution is suspended when such a breakpoint is reached. It may be resumed in the normal way from that point, or debugging may continue using any of the stepping approaches referred to above.

A breakpoint may be set by selecting the statement where it is required, and then using the *Set/Unset Breakpoint* button, shown in Figure 4.4. This specifies where the execution is to be suspended – immediately before that statement is executed. The way in which the statement is executed is not changed. If a breakpoint is no longer needed, it should be removed in the same way: by selecting the statement, and using the *Set/Unset Breakpoint* button. A quicker way of carrying out the same operation is by using the shortcut key, which is *F9*. It has the same effect as the *Set/Unset Breakpoint* button.

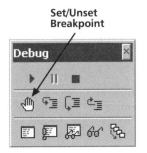

Figure 4.4 Debug toolbar: Set/Unset Breakpoint

Because it is designed for statements which are executed, the breakpoint facility cannot be used on any lines of code which are not executable. Because of this, breakpoints cannot be set on comment lines or declarations, or on blank lines. An active breakpoint is highlighted in the code listing according to the colours set up in the *Editor Format* option of the *Options* menu in the *Tools* command, as introduced in Chapter 2. An example of this is shown in Figure 4.5.

It is important for the programmer to maintain a record of the breakpoints which are present in a Visual Program. The unexpected halting of a program being tested, because of a forgotten breakpoint, can be quite alarming. It is better to remove breakpoints, and reset only those which are needed, to avoid such a problem. If, for any reason, you forget where they have been set, they may all be cleared using the *Clear All Breakpoints* option in the *Debug* menu.

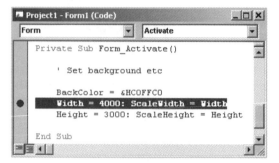

Figure 4.5 Breakpoint indication

Quick test

1. What are the differences between *Step Into*, *Step Round* and *Step Out*?

2. How may all breakpoints be removed from a program being tested?

Variable values

You will learn how to access variables during the execution of a Visual Program.

Whilst it is useful to be able to follow the paths executed during the running of a program, this is not always sufficient for debugging purposes. This may explain why a defective program does not produce the correct results, but without giving reasons **why** incorrect paths are being followed. This will typically depend on the values of the program variables. It is therefore important for a good Development Environment to allow a programmer to inspect the values of the program variables. It is also useful to be able to alter these, under developmental conditions, to allow (for example) calculations to be checked with alternative values of their arguments. This is carried out by the use of the **Watch** facility in the Visual Basic Development Environment.

During the debugging of a Visual Program, the execution may be interrupted for debugging purposes, as described in the previous section. At this time, the values of the program's variables may be displayed using the Visual Basic *Print* method. It is also possible to change the values of those variables, but this should be done with great care. Indiscriminate changes can cause otherwise impossible paths to be taken through a program, thereby making the debugging activity effectively meaningless.

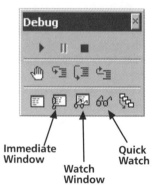

Figure 4.6 Debug toolbar: Immediate Window, Watch Window, Quick Watch

This approach to debugging uses the *Immediate Window*. This appears in the debug toolbar, as shown in Figure 4.6. The option may also be found in the *View* menu; or the *Ctrl + G* shortcut key may be used. This command causes the *Immediate Window* to open. Within this window, simple Visual Basic statements may be typed and executed, and the results of Print statements executed at this time may also be viewed in this window. An example is shown in Figure 4.7.

Figure 4.7 Immediate Window

A breakpoint has been set one line later than that shown in Figure 4.5, and the program executed to that point. The Code window shows this, just above the Immediate Window. The statement Print Width has been typed and obeyed, and given the result 4000 (as expected).

If, for some reason, it had been necessary to change the value of Width to (say) 3000, this might have been done by obeying Width = 3000. This might have had unexpected results, however, unless the value of ScaleWidth had been altered at the same time. It is to avoid this kind of error that great care must be taken.

Unfortunately, such results will not necessarily be shown in the most useful format. For this reason, care should be used when interpreting the results. This is also shown in Figure 4.7, where the value of BackColor has been printed. Although its value was specified in hexadecimal, the unformatted *Print* method has been used, which gives the result in decimal. To demonstrate more easily that it is correct, it has been printed in a friendlier and more appropriate format, as shown here.

─────────── CRUCIAL ACTIVITY ───────────

Set up a small program. Step through some of the instructions. Check the values of some of the variables in the Immediate Window.

An easy way to display the value of a variable is to highlight it in the program code and use the *Quick Watch* button on the debug toolbar. This opens a small window giving the name of the variable and its current value. As shown in Figure 4.8, it also gives the context in which the variable occurs: the name of its procedure or function, with the part of the program in which the corresponding control is found.

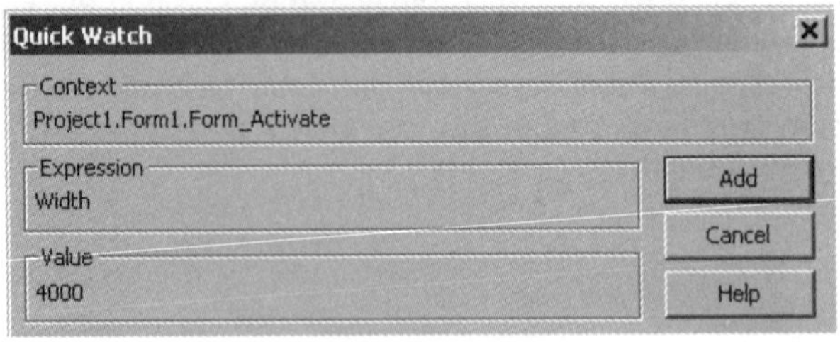

Quick Watch ⊠

Context
Project1.Form1.Form_Activate

Expression
Width

Value
4000

Add

Cancel

Help

Figure 4.8 Quick Watch Window

When the value has been verified, the *Cancel* button allows the execution to be continued. This is thus a straightforward way to make sure that the values of variables are correct. If not, appropriate corrective action must be taken.

Quick test

1. Name two ways of finding the values of variables while a Visual Program is running.

2. What are the disadvantages of using default formatting when displaying variables?

Section 7

How did the program arrive here?

You will learn about the Call Stack display.

The debugging facilities introduced above suppose that the identification of correct program running is going according to a predetermined plan. The steps being taken through a Visual Program have been decided in advance, and the verification of values and program paths is following a suitably formulated test activity. Unfortunately, life does not always cooperate as well as that, and unexpected difficulties can arise.

It is quite straightforward to set a breakpoint in a given part of the code of the Visual Program. If that code is executed, it is obvious *where* the execution of the program has reached. It is not necessarily clear, however, *how* it was reached. There may be more than one position, for example, from which a subroutine or function is called. To allow for a trace of the paths followed within a Visual Program, the *Call Stack* display facility is provided (see Figure 4.9).

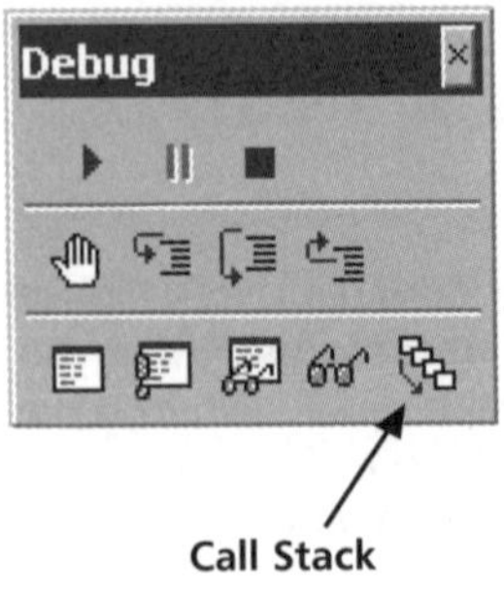

Call Stack

Figure 4.9 Debug toolbar: Call Stack Window

As each procedure is entered, its name is put into this stack. It is a Last-In-First-Out structure, corresponding to the way in which procedures are called. This stack may be displayed to show a trace of procedure calls. An example of this is shown in Figure 4.10, with three procedures in the stack.

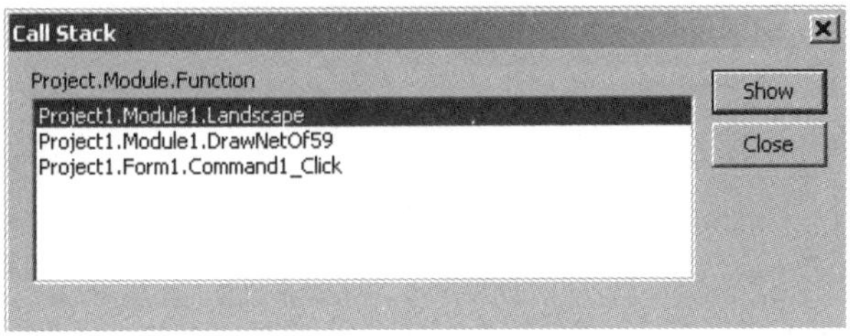

Figure 4.10 Call Stack Window

The top of the stack shows the current procedure, called by the one next below it, and so on. Each is shown as a three-part name: *Project.Module.Function*. In this case the project is Project1, and there are two modules: Form1 and Module1. The three functions (the names of the procedures) are Landscape – the current procedure – which was called by DrawNetOf59, which was in turn called by Command1_Click. In this way, it is possible to determine the route by which a particular place in the program has been reached.

Quick test

1. What are the components in a Call Stack display item?

2. Why is the Call Stack held as a Last-In-First-Out structure?

Section 8

Watching the variable values

You will learn how the values of variables in a Visual Basic program may be monitored.

In a small program, it is not difficult to keep aware about what all variables are doing at all times. It is unlikely that errors in their values will affect a small program without being trapped, although not even small programs are immune to such happenings. When a program becomes larger, however, the possibilities increase of small initial errors leading to large unexpected outcomes. For this reason, among others, extra facilities are available to Visual Programmers using the **Watch** system.

Referring back to the situation in Section 6 of this chapter, a variable has been selected to discover its value at a specific time. If, instead of pressing the *Cancel* button, pressing the *Add* button at this time will add this variable to the watch list. This is a collection of variables whose values are displayed in the *Watch* Window, which opens automatically when a variable is added to the watch list. This window may also be opened using the button on the debug toolbar, shown in Figure 4.6.

CRUCIAL ACTIVITY

Find alternative ways of opening the *Watch* Window.

In the example of the Watch Window shown in Figure 4.11, two variables have been selected and added to the watch list. These are fScalingFactor and fRoot3, both of which hold single length floating point variables. Their respective values are also given. These values will change during the course of the program's execution, and those changes will be kept up to date in the Watch Window.

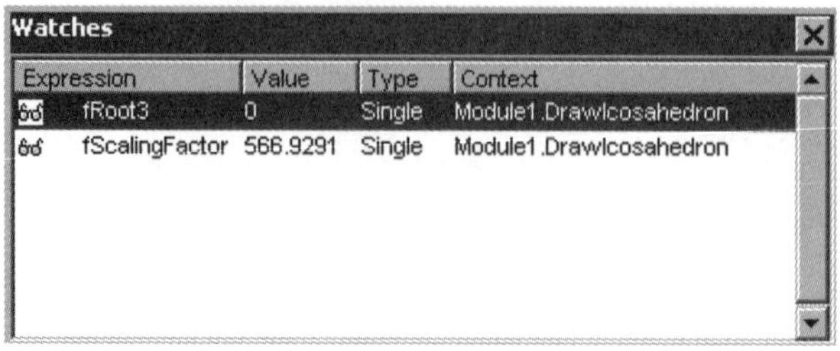

Figure 4.11 Watch Window

There is an advantage in using this approach when there are some variables whose values are of continuing importance during a debugging session. The on-going surveillance which is kept on these variables can be of considerable help during the debugging of a program. But it is in the programmer's interest not to have too many of these, to avoid confusion between a large number of variables.

CRUCIAL ACTIVITY

There is an alternative way of discovering a variable's value during debugging. While a program is halted at a breakpoint, place the cursor over the name of a variable. What happens?

To assist in complex debugging sessions, there is a further facility provided when watching variables. The execution of the program may be halted when a particular expression becomes true, or when the value of a variable changes. This is managed by the explicit specification of a watch variable, using the *Add Watch* option in the *Debug* menu. With the variable `fScalingFactor` selected, this opens the window shown in Figure 4.12. The watch type selected is *Break When Value Changes*. This allows any new value taken by the variable to be checked, no matter where this occurs in the program. While this is often used for individual variables, it may also be applied to an expression.

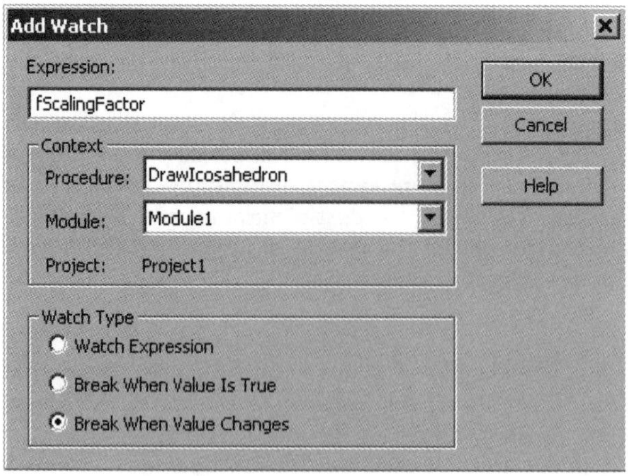

Figure 4.12 Watch Window options

Quick test

1. What information is given about a variable in the Watch Window?
2. What type of variable takes the value *True*?

Section 9

End of chapter assessment

Questions

1. What ways are available to check the values of variables during a debugging session?
2. What is the purpose of a breakpoint, and why is it useful?
3. When is it inappropriate to use a Debugging Environment?
4. Why is the `Option Explicit` statement used?
5. What step facilities are available during Visual Program debugging?
6. What is the purpose of a Call Stack?

Answers

1. The values of variables may be checked using the Immediate Window, which requires explicit actions to be carried out for each variable; the Watch Window, which must be populated, but changes as the variables change (and also provides further information about each variable); and by pointing to a variable in the Code window, which gives value information in a small drop-down window.
2. The statements of a Visual Program are executed until a breakpoint is reached; the execution is then suspended and the session enters debugging mode. This is useful for avoiding explicit program stepping for parts of a Visual Program which have already been debugged.
3. Debugging Environments should be used *only* during debugging. Their facilities have no place in Visual Programs that are working.
4. The `Option Explicit` statement is used to ensure that all variables in a Visual Program have been explicitly declared and specified. This avoids misspellings, leading to uninitialised variables.
5. These are Step **Into**, Step **Round** and Step **Out**.
6. A Call Stack shows the subroutines which currently form part of the (static) execution path of a Visual Program. These are the subroutines which have so far been called, but which have not be exited. This allows a programmer to verify the path a Visual Program has taken during its execution so far.

Section 10

Further reading and research

http://www.dcs.napier.ac.uk/hci/VB30/HTML/debugging.html gives a wide-ranging view of debugging. It is based on earlier versions of Visual Basic, but is nevertheless valuable for its alternative description of material presented in this chapter.

Chapter 5
More about Visual Programming controls

Chapter summary

This chapter describes approaches for producing consistent visual and programming interfaces. It introduces a number of new Visual Programming controls. These include option buttons, check boxes, simple lines and shapes, and scrolling bars and sliders. A worked example is used to show some of the facilities available.

Learning outcomes

This chapter's learning outcomes deal with a wider range of Visual Programming controls and their efficient layout. When you have completed this chapter successfully, you will be able to:

Outcome 1: Space and position Visual Programming controls using the tools provided.

Outcome 2: Use a structured approach for defining sets of tools.

Outcome 3: Specify different ways to allow choices to be made in users' applications.

Outcome 4: Include line and shape controls in a Visual Program.

Outcome 5: Add scrolling and slider controls to a Visual Program for the input of continuous variables.

How will you be assessed on this?

Typically you may be asked to implement more advanced Visual Programs, and describe them using formal reports.

Section 1

Modifying existing controls

In this section, you will learn about other ways to define controls consistently.

When using groups of similar Visual Programming controls, there are two aspects to consider. One is visual, and the other is organisational. The visual aspect has already been introduced in Chapter 3, where consistency of layout is mentioned. This may be done by a careful checking of the size and positioning of each control. To illustrate this, the application developed in Chapter 3 will be used.

There is assistance available for this important part of the design. To ensure that the three buttons whose captions are *Load*, *Save* and *Cancel* are the same size, the *Make Same Size* option is chosen from the *Format* menu, as shown in Figure 5.1. The three buttons are simultaneously selected in the design aspect of the form, and the option is then used.

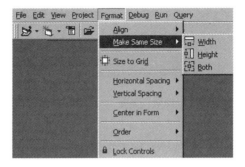

Figure 5.1 Equal control sizing

This may be done in two ways: by defining an outline round them using the mouse, or by use of the *Ctrl* key on the keyboard. To define the outline, consider a rectangle enclosing the buttons, then click and drag the mouse pointer from one corner of this rectangle to the opposite corner. This will select the buttons, and the button on the left, or at the top, will then be used to define the sizes of the others. Using the *Ctrl* key allows controls in different parts of the form to be selected. Click on any one of the controls, then hold the *Ctrl* key down, and click on the others in turn. This selects them all, and the first one selected defines the size for the others.

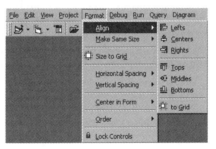

Figure 5.2 Alignment of controls

Once they are the same size, it is still necessary to line them up in a consistent pattern. This may best be done with the assistance of the *Align* option of the *Format* menu, as shown in Figure 5.2. As the buttons are in a vertical row, it is best to align their *Lefts*, *Centers* or *Rights*. These will all have the same effect, in any case, because they have by now all been made the same size. (You will notice the Americanisation of the spelling here.)

─────── CRUCIAL ACTIVITY ───────

Check the application you constructed while you were studying Chapter 3. Use the *Make Same Size* and the *Align* options to check that you had already carried out these actions 'by eye'.

There is another way to ensure that controls which should be the same size are consistent in that way. An example control is set up and selected. It is then copied and pasted. When the paste option is used, the Visual Basic system gives the option of forming a **control array**. For this example, this should not be done (control arrays are dealt with in the next section). A copy of the control appears in the top left of the form, and may then be dragged into the correct position. This may then be repeated as often as necessary. The controls specified are as independent as with the previous method of definition, but are all of the same size.

Quick test

1. What formatting tools are available for producing consistently sized controls?

2. How is the layout grid useful during the design of a Visual Program?

Arrays of controls

In this section, you will learn about using arrays of controls.

Controls in a Visual Program may be set up individually in the same way as program variables in other types of program. However, in the same way that a number of program variables of the same characteristics – for example, all for the storage of real numbers – may be organised into an array, the same may be done for Visual Program controls.

In the same way that variables in an array in any program must have the same type, the controls in a Visual Program array should all have the same general function to perform. In the example introduced in Chapter 3, the three buttons whose captions are *Small*, *Medium* and *Large* are of this type, and will be used in this example.

The first of these is defined, sized, put in its place, and its name and caption are set up. Because these buttons will be treated in a different way, the name chosen on this occasion will be cmdSize. It is then selected, copied and pasted. On this occasion, it is made part of a control array. It is then placed as in the previous example, and given its caption, but it is not renamed. When this is repeated for the third button, the question is not asked a second time, because it is assumed that all copies of this button will be part of the control array. There are therefore three buttons, as before, which may all be positioned as in the example.

The coding to deal with them is not dealt with in the same way as before. Instead of having three separately named buttons to be coded as individuals, there are now three buttons forming a named array, distinguished by their subscripts. The pseudocode design becomes:

cmdSize: If this is element 0 then change text box text size to 8 points
              else if this is element 1 then change text box text size to 10 points
              else change text box size to 12 points
      End if

The design deals with a selection according to which button is pressed. The different outcomes are identified by the array element subscript, which starts at zero. The corresponding Visual Basic code is shown in Figure 5.3.

CRUCIAL CONCEPT

The first element in an array in Visual Basic has subscript 0.

The subroutine activated by the click event for the cmdSize button controls has a parameter, set by the system. It is named Index, and defines which of the buttons in the control array was pressed: 0, 1 or 2. The correspondence between the pseudocode design and the Visual Program code is straightforward. The keywords introduced here deal with selection statements, and are If, Then, ElseIf, Else and End If. Their meanings correspond to those in languages with which you are already familiar.

```
Private Sub cmdSize_Click
        (Index As Integer)
    '

    ' Use of control array
    '

        If Index = 0 Then
            txtEditor.Font.Size = 8
    ' "Small" button
        ElseIf Index = 1 Then
            txtEditor.Font.Size = 10
    ' "Medium" button
        Else
            txtEditor.Font.Size = 12
    ' "Large" button
        End If

    End Sub
```

Figure 5.3 Change font size subroutine, revised

CRUCIAL ACTIVITY

Change the application you created in the work of Chapter 3 to use a command array of buttons in this way.

Quick test

1. What is the largest subscript in a Visual Basic array of ten items?
2. How do control array names differ from controls not in an array?

Section 3

Making choices

In this section, you will learn about the use of option buttons to select from a list of mutually exclusive choices.

The use of command buttons to select a single alternative is effective. This approach uses a small fraction of operations available to such buttons, but is valid. However, there are controls specifically provided to carry out this action. **Option button** controls are designed to select exactly one from a set of possible outcomes. These controls are sometimes called **radio buttons**, after buttons used on radio receivers to select one from a number of possible radio stations.

Option buttons may be placed on a form and sized in the same way as any other controls. They may be formed into control arrays as described in the previous section. An option button may be selected when the Visual Program is running, by clicking on it. That button then has its *Value* property set to *True*. When a group of option buttons is added to a form, however, if one is selected, the others are automatically unselected. This means that only one of the group may be **true** at a time. The previous example corresponds to this situation, and is illustrated in Figure 5.4.

Figure 5.4 Option button controls

CRUCIAL CONCEPT

In a group of option buttons, either one may be selected, or none of them.

It is usually assumed that one of these options should be chosen. This would be specified as a default. This may be activated either at design time or at run time. If this is to be done at design time, the *Value* of the default option button should explicitly be set to *True*. If it is carried out at run time, an early statement in the program, during its initialisation, should be

$$optMedium.Value = True$$

assuming that the default control is named `optMedium`.

While the Visual Program is running, it is possible to change the option selected by clicking on it. This changes its *Value* to *True*, and the *Values* of the others to *False*. This will not be otherwise detected by the Visual Program unless it is specifically tested. It is therefore important to decide when any option change should be acted upon. In the previous implementation of the example program, the use of a command button was detected by the corresponding *Click* event. Option buttons also have *Click* events, and these may be used in the same way. Alternatively, it may be decided to ignore any option change until another event is signalled, and act upon it then. This will depend on the functionality of the Visual Program and its design. A possible coding sequence is shown in Figure 5.5, to be activated by a suitable event.

```
If optSmall.Value Then
    txtEditor.Font.Size = 8
ElseIf optMedium.Value Then
    txtEditor.Font.Size = 10
ElseIf optLarge.Value Then
    txtEditor.Font.Size = 12
End If
```

Figure 5.5 Option button coding

CRUCIAL ACTIVITY

Replace the command button controls in the example program with option buttons. You may wish to make the option buttons into a control array at the same time.

Quick test

1. How is a default value given to an option button?

2. How many option buttons may be selected at the same time?

Further choices

In this section you will learn about making independent and non-exclusive choices.

The selection of one from a set of options is a common requirement in a Visual Program. It is not uncommon to have more than one such choice being made at the same time. An example of this is shown in Figure 5.6, where the choice of text size is independent of the style to be chosen for the text. In this case, bold or normal text are the choices. If all of the option buttons were placed directly in the form, the choices would not be independent. The choice of either *Bold* or *Normal* would nullify any choice of *Text size*.

CRUCIAL ACTIVITY
Try the above, and verify the outcomes.

In the example shown in Figure 5.6, this has been dealt with. Each of the two groups of option buttons is placed in a **frame**. This is a control designed to contain other controls, for this purpose of establishing independence. The frames, in turn, are placed in the form. These two groups of option buttons may now function independently. This can be seen by reference to the two simultaneously selected options. The programming characteristics are unchanged by this approach. It is organisational only.

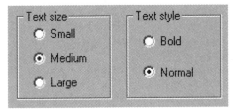

Figure 5.6 Independent option button controls

This selection of the use of bold text is artificial in some respects. It is customary to present three main text styles which are not mutually exclusive. These styles, typically bold, italic and underlined, may appear in up to eight combinations.

CRUCIAL ACTIVITY
Make sure you can identify the eight combinations.

The specification of choices which may appear in different combinations, rather than strictly one at a time, is carried out by the **check box** control. It is placed in a form and sized as for the option button control, but has a different function. Each check box is turned on or off independently of any others which may have been included in the design.

The modification to the example program is shown in Figure 5.7. The check box controls have been placed in a frame for the purposes of visual consistency. This is designed to help the users' understanding of the program. The figure is intended to demonstrate that more than one check box control may be selected at once. Each is therefore shown to be independent of the others.

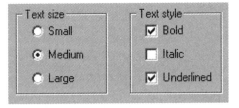

Figure 5.7 Check box controls

CRUCIAL TIP
Make sure you understand the functional differences between option buttons and check boxes.

Quick test

1. How does the use of a frame control affect the way option buttons may be used?

2. What are the differences between option buttons and check boxes?

Section 5

Drawing lines and figures

You will learn how to construct diagrams using shapes and lines.

When constructing visual applications, the drawing objects available can be very effective in producing a good appearance. These include straight lines and several kinds of shapes, in addition to pictures available from illustrations and other stored material. The inclusion of graphic material is a powerful aid to setting a visual scene, but should be used with care. There is no merit in including a picture or a diagram merely because it can be done. The correct use of colours and appropriate sizes of illustration are also important. If there is need to display a warning, it will be sensible to use associated warning colours and pictures. But these should not be used in other situations, or they will lose their strength.

One fundamental diagram control is that of a line. It enables a single line to be drawn between two points, with adjustable colours, thicknesses and designs. This control has no associated events, and is therefore for presentation purposes alone. There are also a number of fundamental shapes available. These include circles, ovals, rectangles and squares. These are functionally similar to lines, being only for the purposes of presentation and appearance.

They may be added to a form at design time, thus being permanent as far as a given Visual Program is concerned. They are selected from the toolbar in the customary way. A line control is added to a form by positioning the cursor at the initial point, and then clicking and dragging the line to its end point. Its layout may be changed afterwards by selecting the line, and then moving either end point. Different lines may be drawn by changing the properties of the line.

─── CRUCIAL ACTIVITY ───

Construct a line on a form. Look at the properties available (there are not many). Experiment with the properties *BorderStyle* and *BorderWidth*. Make sure you take notes about their effects.

Shape controls may be added to a Visual Program using the shape control in the same way. The default shape is a rectangle. It is positioned on a form by clicking on the position of one corner, and then clicking and dragging the cursor to the opposite corner. Its *BorderStyle* and *BorderWidth* properties are similar to those of a line control. It also has a *Shape* property. This allows one of the six possible shapes to be selected.

─── CRUCIAL ACTIVITY ───

Construct a shape control on a form. Make a note of the available shapes.

Alternatively, these lines and shapes may be constructed during the execution of a Visual Program. A typical reason for such a construction might be to display a histogram. This has no active components connected with events, but is to convey information.

A simple line histogram is drawn with the code shown in Figure 5.8. This code is activated by the click event of an associated command button. The `Line` method is called five times to draw five successive bars of a vertical histogram. The (x, y) coordinates of the beginning and ending points on each line are given in parentheses.

```
For iCount = 0 To 800 Step 200
    Line (500 + iCount, 1800 - iCount) - _
                (500 + iCount, 2500)
Next iCount
```

Figure 5.8 Construction of line controls

─────────────────CRUCIAL ACTIVITY─────────────────

Embed the given code in an application and execute it. Check the result.

It is straightforward to draw rectangular boxes using four lines for each. This is a sufficiently common requirement that a modification of the Line method is provided to draw rectangles. The method is used as if to draw a line between opposite corners of a rectangle, but an extra parameter (B for 'box') is added. This modification is shown in Figure 5.9. The two commas are necessary, because there is a (null) parameter also included. Notice the two modifications: the second x-coordinate is not 500, but 600, and the B appears at the end. This produces a rectangle in outline only. If a solid rectangle is preferred, the parameter is changed to BF (for 'box filled').

```
For iCount = 0 To 800 Step 200
    Line (500 + iCount, 1800 - iCount) - _
                (600 + iCount, 2500), ,B
Next iCount
```

Figure 5.9 Drawing histogram rectangles

Quick test

1. What are the six available shapes?

2. How many different *BorderStyle* values are available for lines and shapes?

Using scrolling and slider controls

In this section you will learn about accessing pieces of information that are not immediately visible.

Scroll bars are familiar aspects of a Visual Program. They are usually found to the right side or at the bottom of a part of the screen. They are typically used to access different parts of a window whose contents are not all visible at the same time. This is such a widespread requirement that it forms part of the built-in functionality of a text box. This is addressed before the wider use of the slider control.

In the example implementation constructed in Chapter 3, the text box accepts input either from a file (the *Load* option) or from the keyboard. If there are too many lines of text to fit into the text box, those at the top are moved out of sight. They may be viewed by moving inside the text box using the arrow keys on the keyboard. However, if the words of the text do not fit a line in the text box window, they are reformatted if possible. This is done by 'wrapping' words into enough lines to hold all of the text.

An alternative approach is given by adding a horizontal scroll bar to the text box. To do this, change the text box *ScrollBars* property to *1 – Horizontal*. This has to be done at design time for the application. This helps to demonstrate that the properties associated with controls are divided into two sets. While the values of all of them may be queried at any time, some cannot be changed while the Visual Program is running. They are read-only variables, and must be set using the design view of the text box.

─────── CRUCIAL CONCEPT ───────

Some aspects of a Visual Program must be set during the design stage, and may not be changed while the program is being executed.

Such a scroll bar is intended to simplify the navigation when there is more information than can easily be shown at one time. It does not override the facilities already provided by the keyboard, but does avoid appearing to insert spurious characters into the text file. The text box functionality may be further altered by changing the *ScrollBars* property to *2 – Vertical* or to *3 – Both*.

─────── CRUCIAL ACTIVITY ───────

Insert a horizontal scroll bar into the text box. Verify the changes that are made to the appearance and the functionality of the Visual Program. Verify the changes that take place if you make further alterations.

Sliders are controls which appear similar to scroll bars. They are used to select a particular value from a given range. They provide a visual alternative to typing a value for input into a Visual Program. They have the advantage that limits can be set beforehand, which means that no range checks need to be carried out. They have the further advantage that mistyping cannot give rise to invalid characters or formats being presented, and giving rise to consequent errors.

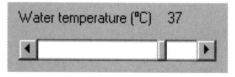

Figure 5.10 Horizontal slider control

An example of this is given in Figure 5.10. The minimum and maximum temperatures allowed are 5°C and 45°C respectively. The slider properties have been set to reflect these values. The display is linked to the position of the slider, and the corresponding value to that position is shown. The code to effect this is shown in Figure 5.11.

```
Private Sub hsbTemp_Change()
'
' Show current temperature
'
    lblTemp.Caption = hsbTemp.Value

End Sub
```

Figure 5.11 Horizontal slider control code

The event which causes the value to be displayed is a completed change in the position of the slider. The value given by the slider is in `hsbTemp.Value` and in the example this is simply transferred to the display field `lblTemp.Caption`. No other changes need be made, as they are all dealt with by the Visual Basic system.

Quick test

1. What kind of control properties cannot be changed while a Visual Program is being executed?

2. What are the advantages of using a slider control to input values?

Section 7

A worked example

You will learn about using a slider to construct a simple picture with shapes.

Previous sections introduced ways of drawing shapes and capturing simple data from a slider. The two are here combined in a simple application to show a clock face, where the time is taken from the value returned by the slider. The time will be taken on the 24-hour clock and displayed both as a digital value in the format hh:mm and as an analogue value in the conventional form.

This will require a certain amount of trigonometry. The formulae used will be presented without a formal derivation, because that is not central to the learning experience at which this text aims.

There are four fixed controls: a form to contain the display, a circle shape to represent the clock, a horizontal slider to generate a number between 0 and 1,439 and a label to display the time in a digital format. The clock's hands are generated dynamically according to the input from the slider control.

```
┌──────────────── CRUCIAL ACTIVITY ────────────────┐
│ Work out why those numbers have been selected. (Hint: how many minutes are there in a day?) │
└───────────────────────────────────────────────────┘
```

Control	Name	Caption
Form	frmClock	The Clock
Horizontal slider	hsbTime	
Label	lblTime	
Shape	shpClock	

Table 5.1 Control types, names and captions

The fixed controls are given names and captions according to the lists in Table 5.1. The *Min* and *Max* properties of the slider are set at 0 and 1439 and the circle shape control is positioned symmetrically. There is no specific requirement to give it a particular position or size, because the clock's 'hands' will deduce their positions according to the position and size of the circle while the Visual Program is being executed.

The event which causes the time to be displayed is a change in the value represented by the slider. This causes entry to the subroutine hsbTime_Change. The initial requirement is to erase the hands displaying the previous time. This is carried out by the method

frmClock.Cls

which clears (Cls) all generated marks from the form frmClock. This is a standard method for erasing generated material from any control acting as a container, such as a form (as in this case) or a frame. It does not remove any markings inserted into the container at design time.

Some constants are then set up, where the value of pi is possibly familiar. This is often needed when carrying out calculations involving circles. The position of the centre of the clock is calculated, with its x-coordinate half of the circle's width from its left point, and its y-coordinate a similar distance below its highest point. This gives values of

shpClock.Left + shpClock.Width / 2
and shpClock.Top + shpClock.Width / 2

respectively. The line representing each clock hand will start at the point whose coordinates are specified by these values, of a given size in a calculated direction.

The 24-hour clock is converted to a 12-hour basis before the hands are displayed. This uses the mod operator to give a value in the range 0 – 719 (note: 720 is half of 1440). The position of the hour hand relative to the centre of the clock is next calculated, and the Line method is used to draw the hour hand. The instruction has the form

Line (iCentreX, iCentreY) – Step(iHourhandX, iHourhandY)

with the following meaning. The x- and y-coordinates of the centre are shown first, in parentheses, followed by a separating '–' and the keyword Step. This informs the Line method that the next pair of coordinates does not form an absolute value, but are given relative to the previous coordinates, which define the centre of the clock face.

Figure 5.12 Clock as displayed

A similar calculation and display is carried out for the minute hand. Finally, the digital form of the time is calculated, formatted and displayed. The code for the event-driven routine of the Visual Program is shown in Figure 5.13. Notice the use of continuation lines for the two Line methods. These are purely for program text layout purposes.

```
Option Explicit

Private Sub hsbTime_Change()
'
' Read time between 00:00 and 23:59
'
Dim iMinutes, iTime As Integer
Dim iCentreX, iCentreY As Integer
Dim iHourhandX, iHourhandY As Integer
Dim iMinhandX, iMinhandY As Integer
Dim dPi, dTheta As Double
Dim sSeparator As String

' Remove old lines
    frmClock.Cls
' Calculate fixed values
    dPi = 3.1415926535
    iCentreX = shpClock.Left + shpClock.Width / 2
    iCentreY = shpClock.Top + shpClock.Width / 2
' Convert 24-hour clock to 12 hours
    iTime = hsbTime.Value Mod 720
' Show hour hand
    dTheta = dPi * iTime / 360
    iHourhandX = shpClock.Width * Sin(dTheta) / 3
    iHourhandY = -shpClock.Width * Cos(dTheta) / 3
    Line (iCentreX, iCentreY)- _
            Step(iHourhandX, iHourhandY)
' Show minute hand
    iMinutes = iTime Mod 60
    dTheta = dPi * iMinutes / 30
    iMinhandX = shpClock.Width * Sin(dTheta) / 2
    iMinhandY = -shpClock.Width * Cos(dTheta) / 2
    Line (iCentreX, iCentreY)- _
            Step(iMinhandX, iMinhandY)
' Show digital time
    sSeparator = '':''
    If iMinutes < 10 Then sSeparator = '':0''
    lblTime.Caption = Int(hsbTime.Value / 60) _
            & sSeparator & iMinutes

End Sub
```

Figure 5.13 Example program code

Quick test

1. What is the effect of the Cls method?

2. What is the effect of the Step keyword in the Line method?

Section 8

End of chapter assessment

Questions

1. What tools are available to assist in generating consistent visual layouts in a Visual Program; and where are they found?
2. What are the advantages of using arrays of controls?
3. What is the best way of organising a group of option buttons to have a consistent effect?
4. How many check box controls may be ticked simultaneously in a group?
5. What are the differences between defining lines and shapes at design time and at run time?
6. What are the main advantages of using slider controls for input of values to a Visual Program?

Answers

1. The *Align*, *Make Same Size* and *Size to Grid* tools are all found in the *Format* menu.
2. Where there are controls of the same type which are also logically connected, they may share their functions if they are organised into a control array. This leads to simpler development, more consistent debugging and more secure programming production.
3. Logical groups of option button should be presented in a *frame* control to identify them, and to prevent them interacting in an unwanted way with any other similar groups.
4. None, or any combination, including all of them: there is no restriction.
5. The properties of lines and shapes defined at design time cannot afterwards be changed during the execution of a Visual Program. This also includes erasing them.
6. Using a correctly defined slider ensures that values of an incorrect type or range can be input into a Visual Program. This removes the need for explicit validation of these aspects of the data.

Section 9

Further reading and research

http://msdn.microsoft.com/library/default.asp?url=/library/en-us/vbcon98/html/ vbconusingvisualbasicsstandardcontrols.asp deals with a large selection of Visual Programming controls.

Chapter 6
Making applications robust

Chapter summary

Approaches to planning to ease problem-solving requirements are followed by reminders and hints about practical considerations in the production of Visual Programs. A useful naming convention is described and illustrated, and further guidance aspects are recommended for the implementation of Visual Programs based on Software Engineering principles. Particular approaches to the design of a user interface are suggested by the use of new controls designed for file specification and access.

Learning outcomes

The learning outcomes of this chapter relate largely to Software Engineering. Following the successful completion of this chapter, you will be able to:

Outcome 1: Describe benefits of forward planning.
Outcome 2: Make recommendations for good programming practice.
Outcome 3: Discuss the need for caution in the development of Visual Programs.
Outcome 4: Use Hungarian Notation for structuring the names of variables.
Outcome 5: Use Software Engineering principles during Visual Program planning and implementation.
Outcome 6: Extend the ways used to access the file system used by a computer application.

How will you be assessed on this?

Typically you may be asked to answer questions about good design and development principles. You may also have to show that you are keeping a careful record of your work. You may have to implement a Visual Program to access the computer's file structure in a well-defined way. You may have to produce program documentation for your Visual Programs.

Section 1

The need for careful planning

In this section you will be reminded about some of the benefits of planning ahead.

There is a word that is behind many of the activities described in this book: it is **professionalism**. It not only implies that any work you do will be done to a high standard. It also means that you will think of others – carefully – when you develop any Visual Programs. This will have many obvious effects. Your work will be appreciated more highly. You will be able to take a justifiable pride in the programs you produce. Programs will have fewer mistakes: with practice, approaching zero errors. There is a saying that 'practice makes perfect'. Never forget that perfection should always be attempted, but may not always be fully realised, unfortunately. But you have to **try**.

CRUCIAL CONCEPT
Nothing is as important as **doing it right**.

That is not all that will happen. Because you will be aiming for and achieving high standards, you will notice that you do less work in the long run. How can this be? Because if you introduce fewer errors during the development of a program, there will be fewer errors to correct before it is completed. If you follow professional standards of production and use professional techniques of development, the outcomes will be more robust.

In the short term, this means that the first approach to solving a problem will not involve you with a computer system. That comes later. The initial thing to do is to **think**. Do you **really** understand the problem you are being asked to solve, or the specification of the Visual Program you have been given to write? If you are not sure, after a reasonable amount of time spent in thought, work out *what* it is that is not understood. Write it down. Discuss it with colleagues. See if there are any aspects of the work which will benefit from research. (Research is not a highbrow way of doing things – it means any approach which will shed some light on the problem.) Look in books, and see what the internet may supply. There are some useful search engines available. If you are following an academic course, ask your instructor, lecturer, teacher or tutor.

Before doing any of these, however, you must remember that to get the right answers (in other words, something that will help to clarify the problem), you have to ask the right questions. If you ask the wrong question, the chance of getting the right answer is very small.

And asking the right size of question is also important. Perhaps you can isolate a small part of the problem, and ask a question – and get the right answer – about that. That will reduce the size of the work still to be done, which might now become fit for solution. Or, perhaps, there may be another small part which can be approached in the same way, again reducing the total of work to be tackled. 'When faced with a problem you do not understand, do any part of it you do understand, then look at it again.'

CRUCIAL TIP
Make sure you keep a careful record of your work. Dates and times are also important, to make sure that you know the sequence of your thoughts, and the successes (and failures) in your work during the process – it has been said that we learn more from our failures than our successes.

It is also important to use the right tools for the solution of problems. Some people work better in words than in diagrams, while others prefer to use pictures, or even a mixture of these two approaches. There is no general 'best' way, but a way which works best for each individual. To assist with finding out such a way, guidelines based on general aspects will be revisited later in this chapter, and extended. Nevertheless, you should check them to discover what is best for **you**.

Quick test

1. How can you make best use of your colleagues when developing applications?

2. Have you started keeping your work record yet? If not, why not?

Section 2

If anything can go wrong, it will

In this section you will learn the importance of archiving your work.

This section has a pessimistic title. Perhaps you do not think that computers are capable of making mistakes? Perhaps you are correct, and anything that fails to work correctly can be traced to other causes. In any case, it is a professional approach to be aware that mistakes can occur, and to guard, as far as possible, against letting their effects spread.

That approach should always be one of caution, and of looking around at each stage of your work to see what might go wrong. You can then take positive action to minimise the effects of any mischance. As a simple example of this, when did you last back your work up? This does not just mean: when did you save your latest program copy? It means, rather, when did you take a copy of **all** of your work? That includes your documentation, copies of your data files and expected results, and all of your program files.

CRUCIAL ACTIVITY

Do it now! Back your work up. It is **always** a good move.

Archiving is an important activity. It provides a sequence of snapshots of the evolution of your work. In this way, you may be able to recreate, if necessary, the steps you took in its development. It should not be done on an 'overwriting' basis, where any material saved merely replaces a previously-saved version. It is important to be sure that you have several copies, even if they are of increasing ages.

They should also be kept **physically** separate. If they are all kept in the same carrying case, and that case disappears, they are all equally useful. That is to say: not very.

You will be lucky if your files take up no more room than will fit on a floppy disk. That is less and less likely, however: many Visual Programs, and especially their documentation, occupy considerable space. You will probably need more room than that provided by a single floppy disk. So you will need to use other media, such as hard drives, or CDs. But back-ups should not **just** be taken to a local hard drive, or through a network, if you are connected to one. Back up to **both**, if you have the opportunity. Better still, if you have a tape (zip) drive, or a CD-writer, back up to either – or, better – both. But that is not enough.

This may sound surprising: now look again at the title of this section. You may imagine that you have successfully written all of your valuable work to a stable medium. Are you prepared to stake all of the effort you have expended in believing in the security of **all** of the links in the chain of your back-up work? Therefore, now check that the files you wrote are the same as the ones you have written them from. Bitter experience has produced many coffee mats which are unreadable CDs, and with the back-up work needed to be done again. But it was far better to find that out at the time, rather than when the back-ups were **really** needed.

CRUCIAL TIP

You can use the file compare program provided with typical operating systems (for example, FC) to check that the copies are the same as the originals. In addition, the author has found other – free! – programs for such comparisons using the World-Wide Web. The programs are not very large; and the effort to find them is well worth it.

Continuing in this pessimistic vein, do you have to submit your work to be assessed? By a particular date? How have you planned for this, in case anything goes wrong? Is your printer **guaranteed** to work just when you need it? Are you **100% sure** that your hard disk drive will not die, just when it is most needed? (Yes, it does happen: not often, but too often.) Always allow longer than you think you will need. Think about Hofstadter's Law, which says: 'It always takes longer than you expect, even when you take into account Hofstadter's Law.'

Quick test

1. When **did** you do **your** last back-up?

2. In what ways can the production of CDs for archives be unstable?

Meaningful names

In this section you will learn about a naming convention designed to reduce programming mistakes.

It is important for many reasons that the names used in a program have a meaning connected with their use in a program. Foremost among these is to reduce the probability of introducing errors. The meaning should be closely related to the task that the variable has to carry out in the program. That meaning should at the same time distinguish between similar uses of similar variables.

It is not enough just to call a counter 'counter'. There may be many counters used in a program: which one is this? It may be in use to step through a list of names – so 'namecounter' would be a better choice. It shows at the same time that it is a counter, and that it is associated with the counting of names.

Do not worry about having too many different variables. The Visual Programming system will make sure that you do not run out of computer storage. If you have so many that you lose track of the purpose of each variable, you have probably given them the wrong names in any case. It is better to be **sure** about the way in which each is being used than to worry about computer system capabilities.

How long should the name of a variable be? There is no correct answer to this: it should be long enough to ensure that it is unique, but not so long that mistakes are likely to be made while it is being input into the Visual Program. It should also be long enough to allow it to describe its use closely.

But it is possible to add a little extra meaning to each variable name which will further decrease the probability of a mistake being made with its use. This is to include, within the name, an indication of what **computer-based** use it will have. Will it be used to store money values, or dates, or strings? If this is done, it is less likely that you, the programmer, will make a mistake in the way in which you use the variables you have selected.

--- CRUCIAL CONCEPT ---

Any method which is liable to reduce the number of programming errors should not be neglected. This can be done by the use of what is known as **Hungarian Notation**. Each name is structured to include an indication of the type of variable to which it refers. This is done, quite simply, by adding a letter or two to the front of each name, according to its type of use.

This approach has already been introduced, with a minimum of explanation, in previous chapters. It will be followed throughout the examples given wherever the programmer has the option to do so. For example, it cannot affect what is done with names defined or specified by other parts of the Visual Basic system. Such system-defined names must be used without modification.

Typical prefixes of this kind as used for variables are shown in Figure 6.1. There are others (the full list stretches into hundreds!), but the ones given here include those used in this book. They all appear straightforward, using the initial letter of the data type as the prefix. The exception is for data type **single**, which has prefix 'f', because 's' is already used for the string data type. This stands for **floating**, which refers to the storage used for single-length variables.

Prefix	Data type	Example
b	Boolean	bGameOver
c	Char	cYesNo
cy	Currency	cyInvoiceTotal
d	Double	dDistance
f	Single	fDiscount
i	Integer	iCounter
l	Long	lCounter
s	String	sName

Figure 6.1 Variable prefixes for Hungarian Notation

(Why Hungarian? Quite simply: the inventor of this approach, Charles Simonyi, came from Budapest, in Hungary. He was influential in its adoption within the Microsoft organisation, although it was first used at an earlier time.)

The 'meaning' part of the variable names are distinguished from their prefixes by starting them with a capital letter. This will not have any effect on the Visual Basic system, but it will help in the readability and understandability of the program as far as you, the programmer, are concerned. Any method that helps the programmer is not to be neglected.

––––––––––– CRUCIAL TIP –––––––––––

Practise the use of Hungarian Notation in other programming languages.

It will not be possible to avoid all errors just by choosing descriptive names. But it will lessen the probability of that happening, which will lead to safer programming techniques. It is not foolproof, but is a **guide** to safer program implementation in the same way that indentation of program text is an indication of program structure.

A slightly different approach, but founded on the same principles, has been used in this book to deal with the special requirements of Visual Basic. The controls used have each been allocated a three-letter prefix, and this will help in reminding you, the programmer, of the reason for each variable, without having to remember it explicitly. These prefixes are given in Figure 6.2.

Prefix	Data type	Example
chk	CheckBox	chkPrint
cmd	CommandButton	cmdYesNo
fra	Frame	fraGender
frm	Form	frmOutline
hsb	HorizontalSlider	hsbDistance
lbl	Label	lblName
opt	Option	optMale
txt	TextBox	txtName
vsb	VerticalSlider	vsbSpeed

Figure 6.2 Control prefixes for Hungarian Notation

This list is not exhaustive, and you have already seen a number of these prefixes, assuming that you are working through this book in sequence. More will be introduced as they are needed, and it is hoped that they will be sufficiently self-explanatory as to require no special mention at those times.

Quick test

1. What would be a reasonable name for a weekly wage, using Hungarian Notation?
2. What kind of errors will a variable naming convention reduce?

Section 4

Software Engineering principles

You will be reminded about some guidelines for producing viable Visual Programs.

When producing a Visual Program, certain principles should always be observed. These include but are by no means limited to attention to design, robustness, maintainability, quality control and assurance and so on. Collectively they are addressed by the concepts of Visual Programming viewed as an engineering discipline. This is another aspect of the professionalism mentioned at the start of this chapter, and is referred to as Software Engineering.

This style of approach means that a considerable amount of work needs to be done before a single line of program code is produced. This may appear unexciting, but it leads to a reduction in the **total** amount of work done on any one system; and carefully applied, to less work being needed where a number of similar systems are to be implemented.

The worst kind of work, however, is that required – often urgently – when a disappointed user points out the deficiencies in a Visual Program which has already been delivered. This can be minimised, and even avoided, by attention to particular aspects of Software Engineering which appear with hindsight to be common sense. This type of corrective maintenance is described in context below.

CRUCIAL TIP

Check carefully: is common sense really common?

It is not the place of this text to spend a long time on the details of Software Engineering. A few important aspects only will be looked at, with a view to minimising the total effort expended in any Visual Program implementation. As the King of Hearts says in *Alice's Adventures in Wonderland*, by Lewis Carroll: 'Begin at the beginning, and go on till you come to the end: then stop.' These are two important pieces of advice: to begin at the beginning, and to stop when you come to the end.

Therefore it is important to identify where the beginning **is**. This will probably consist of a specification of a Visual Program, although this may be part of the production process. In any case, it is most important to be clear what it means. This is not always necessarily what **you** think it means, but what its **originator** thinks it means. If there is any doubt at all about the meaning of any part of a specification, it must be clarified. One sure way of expending too much effort and energy is in carrying out work which was not intended.

CRUCIAL TIP

If in doubt, ask. If in no doubt, check. And do it **carefully**. It might appear boring, but it saves work.

After the specification comes the design. Use any tools which help, or which are required, but do not use tools merely because they are there. It is sometimes more effective to draw diagrams than to use the latest and most advanced packages which appear to do the same thing, but which take much longer. However, in the same way that verification of the intention of a specification is important to save work, clarity in design will also pay off. It is worth checking with the originator of the specification, if that is possible, that the design which is intended to be used is actually a solution of the stated problem. Some things are more frustrating than a carefully designed and implemented solution to the wrong problem, but not many.

While a Visual Program is being designed, look for common activities. These may have been written and tested in a previous application. There is no shame – quite the contrary – in reusing already tried-and-tested program code. But if it is somebody else's, please be sensitive and ask for permission. Then add comments in the program code to this effect. That is the professional approach to code reuse.

It may be necessary to make up all of the program code from scratch, but there may still be items occurring repeatedly within the program. These are best implemented as subroutines or functions, and tested once and once only, rather than being copied and tested many times. Identification of common sub-elements saves time and trouble. This is another aspect of **code reuse**.

Once the design for the Visual Program has been constructed, it should be checked. At this time, certain possibilities will suggest themselves about things to be tested, and ways of testing them. During this process make notes about the testing which will be needed, and why. These notes will help when more formal verification of the implementation is needed. The outcome of this stage should be a design for the actual problem to be solved, and data for the testing process, with reasons for each test. The advantage of this approach is that if any of the tests fail and the Visual Program has to be amended, the reasons for the tests will assist in directing the ways in which the corrections should be carried out.

While you are writing the program code, make sure that explanatory comments are included as a matter of course, and at the time of writing. When the time comes to make changes – not **if**, but **when** – those comments will be very valuable. Therefore their quality should be high, and they should be as clear as possible. Whilst the initial programmer may be called upon to make changes, it may equally be someone else who has to do that work. Put yourself in their place. Is your Visual Program code **maintainable**?

Three kinds of maintainability have been identified, known as:

- **corrective**
- **perfective**
- and **adaptive**.

Corrective maintenance takes place during development of the Visual Program, to correct any errors found. Unfortunately, this continues to be required in some cases when applications have been released to their users; but this should be at a minimum. Perfective maintenance is intended to improve performance at any time. Adaptive maintainability takes place as the environment of the Visual Program changes, for example if a new operating system becomes available for its use.

When the implementation is taking place, and different possible ways of doing the required tasks present themselves, do not always choose the easiest or the shortest. Rather, choose the way that is least likely to fail for any reason; or, having failed, has enough information available to enable the debugging process to be done easily and efficiently. There may be some extra variables holding such useful information **just in case**, but which are never otherwise used. It is far better to have unneeded information than **not** having the information when it is needed. In this way, Visual Programs are **robust**.

Another aspect of this is at a more detailed level, but is helpful in avoiding potential problems. Routines and controls should have only as much data supplied to them as they need. If any more is made available, it may be corrupted by mistake. Further, such implementation units should attempt to be as self-contained as possible. The processes of **information hiding** and **encapsulation**, while widely practised in object orientated applications, also apply to Visual Programming. Ways in which this principle may be extended to have this particular relevance are explored in Chapter 8.

Make sure that all tests are carried out carefully. Do not 'economise' on this aspect of production. It takes much more work to correct parts of a Visual Program which were not tested properly than to test them properly in the first place. The aims are **correctness** and **fitness for purpose**.

In particular for Visual Programs, make sure that the interface presented to the user is consistent. Similar functions should have similarly corresponding controls to carry them out. The information needed by a user to gain maximum benefit from the Visual Program should be present where it is needed and when it is needed, for satisfactory **user friendliness**.

Quick test

1. What individual Software Engineering characteristics have been emphasised in this section?

2. Draw a 'waterfall' diagram describing the process of producing a well-engineered Visual Program.

Section 5

Friendly visual interfaces are safer

You will be introduced to controls used in filename handling.

When designing a Visual Program, the user's interface is important. It is the pathway through which information flows in both directions. For this reason, a good approach to organising that information flow reduces the likelihood of errors during the execution of a Visual Program. This is important in the example used in this section, because the original specification was presented in terms of the user's interface. This will be changed, but in an informal and evolutionary way.

As an example of this approach, consider the simple text editor introduced in Chapter 3. In this chapter this will be extended in two stages, and two new controls will be introduced to help in the design of the visual interface. The first of these is the **drive list box** control. As its name implies, it relates to the drives which the computer system is able to access, such as the floppy disk drive, the hard disk drives, and any CD-ROM or DVD drives.

Because the list of the available drives is known to the computer operating system at any time, it is more difficult to specify an incorrect drive identifier. With careful checking, any fault will become the responsibility of the Visual Programmer, rather than the user. This is significantly safer than the situation which applies to the text editor in its present implementation.

The interface will be extended by two controls: one label and one drive list box. The extra part is shown in Figure 6.3. It is then necessary to take the extra information available and put it to use. This is found in the *Drive* property of the drive list box, and is the name of the disk drive which is currently selected.

The control is a drop down list, where the current selection appears in the box, as shown, but a menu of alternatives is made available if the arrow button to the right of the box is clicked. This gives the drive letter of each available drive, with its name. In Figure 6.3, drive i: is currently selected, with the name [*DATA*]. It is this information which is returned from the *Drive* property.

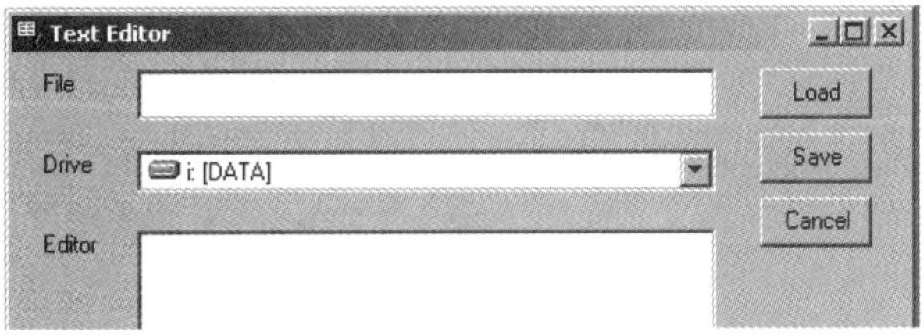

Figure 6.3 Drive list box

It therefore needs to be edited before it can be used. Only the first left-hand character of the string needs to be used. This can be accessed by use of the Left method, which returns the substring of the leftmost n characters, where n is the second parameter of the method. In this case, only one character is needed, so that the filename used in the editor program code is given by

```
Left(drvDisc.Drive, 1) & ":\" & txtFile.Text
```

which produces a string of the form 'i:\Ed.txt' by concatenation. This means that the string holding the filename should be replaced by this string in the two places where it appears, after the Open keyword.

CRUCIAL CONCEPT

The more directed a user's choice can be made, the less likelihood there is for error.

There is, however, a further powerful tool available for accessing files and folders. This is the **Directory list box** control, which is used to specify a particular folder or directory. Its appearance is shown in Figure 6.4, which represents a further amendment to the editor.

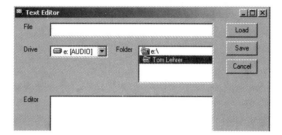

Figure 6.4 Directory list box

It is used in conjunction with the drive list box, and displays a list of the folders available in a given drive or folder. It represents a folder structure hierarchy, and returns a string describing a complete pathway using its *Path* property.

This property is used both as an input parameter to the directory list box control, and to deliver the path which is currently selected. Therefore, to allow the user to carry this out, whenever the required drive is changed, the directory list box must be updated to correspond to this change. There are two changes to the program code needed to deal with both of these design changes.

The first deals with what has to be done when the drive letter changes. This is carried out by the *Change* event handler associated with the drive list box, which is called whenever the drive letter is changed. This needs to inform the directory list box control that the folder path now starts at a different place. The program code for this is shown in Figure 6.5.

```
Private Sub drvDrive_Change()
'
' Update directory list box detail
'
    dirFolder.Path = drvDrive.Drive

End Sub
```

Figure 6.5 Drive change routine

The second change affects the filename string once again. Because the drive letter now forms part of the string returned by the *Path* property, the filename string becomes simpler:

```
dirFolder.Path & txtFile.Text
```

is sufficient at this point. But once again, you have to remember to make this change twice. That is a weakness, and will be dealt with in the near future.

CRUCIAL ACTIVITY

Carry out the changes described, and observe the changes in the behaviour of the editor.

The warnings were given in Chapter 3 that there is no such thing as a small change, and that it is dangerous to change a Visual Program without careful attention to detailed design. The amended Visual Program will work, as long as the file name given in the filename box is valid. It may now be simpler, because there is no need to give a full pathname. However, the facility remains if the user likes typing long names.

But for a robust approach, there are still two sets of operations that should be carried out. It is still far too easy to get out of step if changes are made to any of the three components of the filename: the drive, the folder within the drive or the filename in that folder. And even if the structure of the filename is valid, it may not exist, and therefore will be able to be read; or it may already exist and therefore be overwritten when the file is saved, if it had not been loaded previously. It has further been assumed that the filename specified by the user is valid in format, but no validation of this has taken place. One of these issues will be attended to immediately below. The other will be left for a later occasion, in Chapter 10.

CRUCIAL TIP

Be suspicious. It pays off every time.

Attention will first be given to keeping all parts in step. The clue about managing this easily is the word 'changes' in the previous paragraph. In parallel with the *Change* event handler for the drive list box, there are similar handlers for the directory list box and the text box. And it is now time to deal with the weakness associated with multiple updates of the same string whenever a change is needed to the filename.

A single location will be used to hold the composed filename. This should be declared outside all of the subroutines, in the same part of the program code as `Option Explicit`. It will be set to the filename `dirFolder.Path & txtFile.Text` in the subroutine `dirFolder_Change` and `txtFile_Change`, and added to the subroutine `drvDrive_Change`. It can then be used as the filename in both `Open` methods. Now everything will be kept in step.

Quick test

1. What extra information in addition to the drive letters does the drive list box give?
2. What events are signalled when amendments are made to controls?

Section 6

End of chapter assessment

Questions

1. What information is available from a directory list box?
2. Correctness and robustness have already been identified as desirable characteristics for an application. Name some others which are also appropriate.
3. There are other controls not described in Figure 6.2. Suggest suitable prefixes for these.
4. Will the use of Hungarian Notation stop errors connected with variable names?

5. How often should back-ups be taken?
6. What sources of useful information are available to developers of Visual Programs?

Answers

1. A directory list box provides a string representing the path leading to the folder currently selected, including the drive letter. This needs only a \-separator and a basic filename to form a completely qualified path leading to a given file.
2. A partial list includes completeness, conciseness, consistency, integrity, maintainability, portability, reliability, reusability, testability, understandability and usability. Many more have been identified, but these are arguably the main ones.
3. Reasonable prefixes for the following controls are suggested: `drv` for a drive list box; `dir` for a directory list box; `cbo` for a combo box; `lst` for a list box. There are more.
4. Reasonable naming conventions cannot remove the occurrence of errors connected with improper or incorrect use of those names. Correct use of them can, however, reduce the incidence of such errors.
5. File back-ups should be taken whenever a significant amount of work has been done, and formally at fixed intervals. The larger the back-up, the less likely they are to be taken, and the more important they are likely to be. The appropriate style of back-up should be used in each case: full, partial / incremental, integrated media, separate media, non-updateable media are possible attributes.
6. Material may be found, among other places, in manuals, other books, periodicals, tutor-provided notes, help files, discussion panels and from the World-Wide Web.

Section 7

Further reading and research

http://support.microsoft.com/default.aspx?scid=KB;EN-US;Q173738& deals with specific Hungarian Notation aspects of Visual Programming.

Brooks, Frederick, P. Jr. (1979). *The Mythical Man-Month: Essays on Software Engineering*, Addison-Wesley. ISBN 0-201-00650-2.

Leigh, David *et al.* (1987) *Software: Design, Implementation and Support*, Paradigm. ISBN 0-948825-60-X.

Chapter 7
Other Visual Programming approaches

Chapter summary

The chapter introduces ways in which self-contained Visual Programming processes may be implemented directly in different ways.

Learning outcomes

The learning outcomes of this chapter deal with other approaches to Visual Programming. When you have finished this chapter successfully, you will be able to:

Outcome 1: **Apply further Software Engineering principles to small Visual Programs.**
Outcome 2: **Construct simple user interfaces using VBScript and HTML.**
Outcome 3: **Use variants for the storage of variables.**
Outcome 4: **Use dot notation to qualify different methods at the same time.**
Outcome 5: **Develop macros in other applications.**

How will you be assessed on this?

Typically you may be asked to write a Visual Program using alternative methods of input and output. You may also write stand-alone Visual Programs using alternative implementations. You may be asked to enhance existing applications by introducing Visual Programming techniques. You may have to answer questions about choosing between different storage methods.

Section 1

Alternative areas for Visual Programming

In this section you will learn about other applications where Visual Programming techniques may be used.

There are also other environments where Visual Programs may be found. These include World-Wide Web pages, Word documents and Excel spreadsheets, but they are not limited to those places. These will be used in this chapter as examples of the ways in which Visual Basic is used in a wider context.

─── CRUCIAL CONCEPT ───
Visual Programs may be embedded in other applications.

To do this, some new Visual Basic features will be introduced. These will include the

Message Box and the extended identification feature (dot notation). They apply equally to the Visual Programs already produced, and so may be used within existing applications. There are some aspects which apply specifically to programs developed outside the formal Visual Basic system, which will be introduced for more completeness.

These features are intended to be easy to apply. This may suggest that they may be inserted into a Visual Program wherever it appears appropriate. This may, however, be a dangerous approach. As with other powerful features, they must be used with care, and only after due thought. Inserting such methods without planning leads to unstructured programs, and makes it very difficult indeed to construct worthwhile robust applications.

Having said this, though, when used properly they can give great assistance to application constructors. The essential approach is to use care in the planning of their inclusion. Because they involve text messages and other communication-to-users features, these must be constructed to be clear to those users. The temptation to use concise messages, to save time for the programmer, must be avoided if it leads to users' confusion. As with any aspect of the user interface, thorough planning pays off handsomely.

Quick test

1. What other applications may use Visual Basic?

2. Why may powerful applications be dangerous?

Section 2

Self-contained messages

In this section, you will learn about the Visual Basic Message Box.

It is sometimes convenient for a Visual Program to communicate quickly with a user. This is often done using a Message Box. Message Boxes are almost certainly already familiar. Figure 7.1 shows a typical example, for sending a simple message to the user. There are three parts in this example: a title, a message and a command button. The title is '*VB Script Example*', the message is '*This is a Message Box*', and the button has the legend '*OK*'.

Figure 7.1 Message Box

This has been produced with the Visual Basic method

Msgbox "This is a Message Box", , "VB Script Example"

which shows two of its three components plainly. The statement is identified by *Msgbox*, which takes three parameters – in this case, two of them are explicit. The first is the prompt, and the third is the title to be used for the message box. The second has been left blank in this example, as shown by the missing parameter between the delimiting commas. The reason it has been omitted is because the use of a single *OK* button is so common that this is the default. As no result is expected here, the method has been called as a subroutine.

This message box method may be used wherever a statement is acceptable in Visual Basic, and will normally suspend execution of the Visual Program until it is acknowledged – in this case by clicking the *OK* button. There are variations and extensions on the facilities discussed here. Some of the main features will be described below; but there are many others, and it is left as an exercise to explore these possibilities.

―――――――――――――――― CRUCIAL ACTIVITY ――――――――――――
Check the *Help* file for Message Boxes in the Visual Basic system.

There are three main ways in which Message Boxes may be configured: by the number and type of buttons displayed, by the explanatory icon which may also be shown, and by the default configuration associated with the available buttons. These ways are specified by suitable choices for the Message Box's second parameter, as mentioned above. It is expected that the prompt and the title will be specified in such a way as to be helpful to the user. The possible values are shown in three groups, as in Table 7.1.

Button group	Icon group		Default group
vbOKOnly	*vbCritical*	❌	*vbDefaultButton1*
vbOKCancel			*vbDefaultButton2*
vbAbortRetryIgnore	*vbQuestion*	❓	*vbDefaultButton3*
vbYesNoCancel	*vbExclamation*	⚠	*vbDefaultButton4*
vbYesNo			
vbRetryCancel	*vbInformation*	ⓘ	

Table 7.1 Message Box options

In each case, only one option should be chosen from each group – any other approach may lead to unexpected errors. For the button group, the names describe the number and type of button to be shown (except for *vbOKOnly*, which shows the single button *OK*). In this way, *vbOKCancel* shows two buttons, called *OK* and *Cancel*. This has been used in Figure 7.2. The icon to be shown is given in the icon group (*vbQuestion* in Figure 7.2), and the button used as the default (for example, by pressing the *Enter* key) is defined from the default group.

―――――――――――――――― CRUCIAL ACTIVITY ――――――――――――
Find out what happens if the default chosen is not present – for example, choosing *vbDefaultButton4*.

It is possible in this way to define a message box with OK and Cancel buttons, where Cancel is the default, showing a Question icon, by using the options *vbOKCancel*, *vbQuestion* and *vbDefaultButton2*. These are added together, and placed as the second parameter. The result of this is shown in Figure 7.2, called by the method

Msgbox "Continue from here", vbOKCancel + vbQuestion + vbDefaultButton2,
"Button Example"

The Visual Program is resumed after a Message Box has been displayed by clicking on one of the buttons. But which button has been 'pressed'? This is communicated to the Visual

Program by treating the Message Box method as a function. The value returned depends on which button has been pressed.

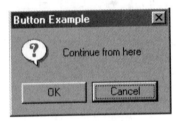

Figure 7.2 Possible Message Box options

To call the method as a function, rather than as a subroutine, the arguments are enclosed in parentheses, and the value is assigned to a variable. A typical function call to this method will therefore appear similar to the following:

iResult = Msgbox ("Continue from here?", vbYesNo + vbQuestion, "Query Example")

This displays a Message Box with two buttons (*Yes* and *No*) and a question mark icon. The value assigned to iResult depends on which button is pressed. It is then up to the programmer to decide which actions to take according to the option chosen.

The possible outcomes are shown in Table 7.2. It is to be hoped that they explain themselves without further description.

vbOK	vbCancel	vbAbort
vbRetry	vbIgnore	vbYes
	vbNo	

Table 7.2 Message Box results

It is important to understand that methods cannot be called interchangeably as subroutines and as functions. Each approach must be used in the correct situation, and specified in the correct way. When calling *Msgbox* as a subroutine, without needing to know which button has been pressed to continue the execution of the program, brackets must not be used. Correspondingly, if it is important to know which button caused the program to continue, *Msgbox* must be called as a function, using brackets, and its value must be assigned to a variable or used in an expression.

Quick test

1. How many buttons can be displayed in a Message Box?

2. What is the difference between a method called as a subroutine and a method called as a function?

Section 3

Visual Basic Script

In this section you will be introduced to Visual Basic Script (VBScript).

There are other places where Message Boxes may be used. These are in stand-alone applications using VBScript: short for 'Visual Basic Script'. They consist of simple files containing the text of short Visual Basic programs, identified with the extension .*VBS*. When executed, they carry out their defined tasks in the same way as any other programs. But they do not need the support structure which other Visual Programs require, being supported directly by the Microsoft Windows Script Host within the operating system. If your operating system does not support VBScript, it is probably available from the World-Wide Web. The support file is called *SCRRUN.DLL* in the Microsoft Windows operating systems.

To execute a VBScript program requires the usual organisation. The necessary instructions have to be input into a file, and that file has to be prepared for execution by the computer system. The instruction for an example application has already been shown: it was

Msgbox "This is a Message Box", , "VB Script Example"

This should be input into a file as simple text, and saved with a file extension of .*VBS*. It is then ready to be executed.

That will immediately suggest the type of execution that the operating system will use. There is no complex requirement to compile or link the program: so it will be interpreted. The .*VBS* extension informs the operating system to use the *SCRRUN.DLL* interpreter in this case. The icon used by the Windows operating system for VBScript files will be displayed for this file as a reminder to the programmer and the user. This is shown in Figure 7.3.

Figure 7.3 VBScript icon

VBScript was developed for use in Active Server Pages for the World-Wide Web. This was so that simple programs could be executed directly within a client's computer system, without referring to the web server. This saves time and cost.

What kind of applications might benefit from such an approach? Typically that kind of processing that might be done quickly and easily on data input into a World-Wide Web page by a user, without reference to any outside application. A straightforward example is in data validation. If an input field is obligatory in an application, but has not been submitted, it is easy to detect. This may be carried out locally without sending an entire input submission to a server for it to be rejected. This approach may also be used to compress data for such submission, thus saving time and cost in a different way.

This is a powerful language. It can carry out operations within a computer's operating system in the same way as any other application. Its use within the World-Wide Web is therefore important, and it can be used to develop meaningful programs even within small files.

But with this power comes potential danger. Computer viruses can be developed and spread using VBScript, and there are many examples of this unhelpful practice. It shows that you should be aware of this possibility, and only allow trusted VBScript applications to be executed. Any file received with a *.VBS* extension should be treated with extreme caution unless you are **100% certain** that it is safe.

CRUCIAL TIP

Powerful languages may also be dangerous if not used carefully, responsibly and professionally.

This application, however, is safe. It is a short example to show that a Visual Program may be embedded within a World-Wide Web page. It uses a *MsgBox*, but this may be exchanged for any valid sequence of VBScript statements. There are some standard items which need to be added before a web browser (for example, Internet Explorer) can accept the VBScript, because World-Wide Web pages use HyperText Markup Language (HTML). The file to be used is shown in Figure 7.4.

```
<HTML>
<SCRIPT LANGUAGE="VBScript">
        MsgBox "This is a Message Box",, "HTML example"
</SCRIPT>
</BODY></HTML>
```

Figure 7.4 HTML embedding

There is only one VBScript statement, starting *MsgBox*. The first line, *<HTML>*, tells the web browser where the HTML program starts, and the next line that VBScript, rather than any other scripting language, is to be used. The instruction *</SCRIPT>* signals the end of the VBScript program, and the last line tells the web browser that there is nothing else to follow. This file should be saved with a *.HTM* extension, so that it is executed with the correct browser.

CRUCIAL ACTIVITY

Make up a file as in Figure 7.4 and execute it.

Quick test

1. How may simple stand-alone Visual Programs be developed?
2. What does HTML stand for?

Section 4

Different methods of output

You will learn how to use further scripting facilities in a variety of ways.

There are other ways in which information may be passed to a World-Wide Web user using VBScript. If there is a large amount of information to be formatted and displayed, the Write method may be used. It is sensible that any **predetermined** text to be displayed would use HTML directly, being more efficient. But using the Write method on its own is not enough: the Visual Program has to know **where** to write the information.

When a web browser displays a page, that page is assumed to be the current document. This is the destination of any information to be presented. But it is necessary to inform the Visual Program about this. This is carried out by qualifying the `Write` method with the place where the output is to be positioned.

The 'dot notation' allows this. Each place within a Visual Program which can accept output may be written to at any time. So far, the active control has been chosen by default – this is the most common way of selecting an output position. If this is to be overridden for some reason, as in the present situation, the destination must be stated explicitly. This is done by specifying its name before the method to be used – in this case `Write` – and separating the two parts by a dot.

CRUCIAL CONCEPT

A method may access a Visual Program control either **explicitly** using the dot notation, or by **default**.

The destination for this World-Wide Web page is `Document`. The method must therefore be qualified as `Document.Write`. An example of this is shown in Figure 7.5. Again, the file extension should be *.HTM*.

```
<HTML>
<SCRIPT LANGUAGE="VBScript">
        Document.Write "This is an example of the Write method"
</SCRIPT>
</BODY></HTML>
```

Figure 7.5 HTML embedding – second example

CRUCIAL ACTIVITY

Make up a file as in Figure 7.5 and execute it.

As a further demonstration of the facilities provided by VBScript, an example will be given which uses a variable. This may be done, as in other Visual Basic programs, by using the `Dim` statement. There is, however, a fundamental difference between other Visual Basic programs and those written with VBScript. The variables used in VBScript are not **typed**: that is to say, they may hold any kind of variable, whether it be a string, an integer, currency, or any valid construction. This is known as a variant. Whilst this may appear to make program construction easier, it imposes an extra burden on the programmer to avoid mistakes. This is an instance where the use of Hungarian Notation may be employed to lessen the chances of such errors. The use of `Option Explicit` will lessen still further the likelihood of problems due to misspellings and similar difficulties.

CRUCIAL CONCEPT

A variable which is not given an explicit type is called a **variant**.

The program is shown in Figure 7.6. It uses two strings and an integer. The integer is given the value of the current month, which is then used to decide the present season (not quite arbitrary, even in the UK). The string `sCrlf` is given a value corresponding to a newline in printing, and the result is constructed in the string `sResult`. The system date is used to give the current month using the methods `Month` and `Now` in combination. The current date is shown directly, using the `Date` method without any explicit parameter.

The `Select Case/End Select` construction is used to decide which season corresponds to a given month. The parameter used is the month number, calculated as described above, in the range 1 to 12. If this has a value of 3, 4 or 5, `sResult` is set to the string

Spring, with similar values used for Summer and Autumn. Any other value is selected by Case Else, as it is assumed to be Winter! The string concatenation operator & is used to combine the separate substrings into one complete result string, as shown.

```
Option Explicit
Dim sCrlf, sResult

' This program computes the current season

sCrlf = Chr(13) & Chr(10) ' Newline
Select Case Month(Now)
Case 3, 4, 5
    sResult = "Spring"
Case 6, 7, 8
    sResult = "Summer"
Case 9, 10, 11
    sResult = "Autumn"
Case Else
    sResult = "Winter"
End Select

' Construct output string
sResult = "It's " & sResult & sCrlf
sResult = sResult & "Calculated at " & Date ()
MsgBox sResult,, "What season is it?"
```

Figure 7.6 VBScript using variables

--- CRUCIAL ACTIVITY ---

Look up any parts of this example program with which you are not familiar. Make notes.

The program was run with a system date set as shown. The result is shown in Figure 7.7. The output was as might be expected, and the weather outside the window immediately changed to reflect the answer. Or perhaps that was wishful thinking. Computer systems have no great effect on the weather, although the converse is not necessarily true.

Figure 7.7 Use of variables

Quick test

1. What values may a variant variable take?

2. How is the destination for text output by the Write method specified?

Section 5

Other methods of input

In this section you will be shown a simple method for inputting a line of text.

The interface described above is satisfactory for simple applications where there are only limited possibilities of choice for users to give information. This is the case where data may be provided by the computer system being used, or where there is a small range of choice of outcomes given to the user by the programmer. This corresponds to the principle that applications should be kept as simple as possible – as far as the user is concerned – to minimise the chance of error. This is also known as *KISS*, which stands for 'Keep It Simple, Stupid'. It is not a reflection on the ability of the Visual Programmer, but a good approach to program design. It is based on a precept over 600 years old, popularly known as Occam's Razor, due to William of Occam. This says that you should always use the **simplest** available approaches to problem-solving. Always provided, of course, that the solution given is one which corresponds to the problem which has been given. (If you look up 'Occam' you may find its spelling is given as 'Ockham'. In the 14th century spelling was much more flexibly approached than it is today!)

CRUCIAL CONCEPT

Never multiply root causes unnecessarily.

Sometimes, however, more information might be needed from the user. As the foundation for an example, a simple text string will be read from the user's input and echoed as output. The VBScript for this example is given in Figure 7.8. A line of text is to be read, as specified by the user. This text is then displayed, so that the correctness of the program can be verified.

```
' Declare variables to be used
Option Explicit
Dim sInput, sTitle, sMessage

' Set up input
sTitle = "VBScript : example use of Inputbox"
sMessage = "Do you want to change the default message?"
sInput = Inputbox (sMessage, sTitle, "Default message")

' Check output
MsgBox sInput, vbInformation, "Output verification"
```

Figure 7.8 Example using Inputbox

The line containing the Inputbox method shows how it is to be called as a function delivering a result, with up to three parameters. Each of these parameters and result is a text string, as indicated by the names given and their usages. The parameters are, in order, the explanatory message to be shown, the title to be displayed for the Inputbox, and a text string to be used as a default. The result of using this method is shown in Figure 7.9.

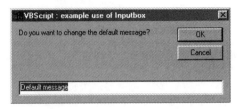

Figure 7.9 Display using `Inputbox`

It shows the strings and the positions in which they are displayed, and the other aspects of the `Inputbox` method. The two buttons are shown by default, with the *OK* button expected. This suggests the tests which have to be applied to verify the usage of this program. There are two possible states to the text message, either leaving the default in place, or changing it by typing an alternative message. There are then at least four ways of continuing: selecting either the *OK* button, or the *Cancel* button, or pressing the *Return* key, or closing the `Inputbox`.

CRUCIAL ACTIVITY

Carry out the testing suggested to find out the effect in each case.

Quick test

1. What happens if the default message in an `Inputbox` is not changed?

2. What is the importance of Occam's Razor?

Section 6

Visual components in Word documents

In this section you will be shown some of the Visual Basic methods associated with Microsoft Word.

Visual Programming elements may also be used in other applications. In the Microsoft Word processor, they are included in specialised methods called **macro**s. A Word macro may be developed in several ways, but may most easily be created using the *Macro* option from the *Tools* menu of Word.

To introduce the code statements which are available, a simple macro will be constructed. It will consist of those methods needed to change the style of the previous word typed to **bold**. This may be done by the standard key or mouse actions. But if these particular actions are to be carried out many times, it is easier to record the sequence of actions, and attach a name to them. Each time they are required, that macro is executed, without need to carry out the actions explicitly.

The cursor is positioned at the beginning of a word, and the *Record New Macro* command from the *Macro* option of the *Tools* menu is started. The macro name is defined, and a shortcut key may be attached to the macro at this time, as shown in Figure 7.10. (This is recommended: it is a very convenient way of executing a macro.) The small icon menu shown in Figure 7.11 is then used to record the macro. The keystrokes to be recorded are carried out, and macro recording is stopped, using the appropriate button.

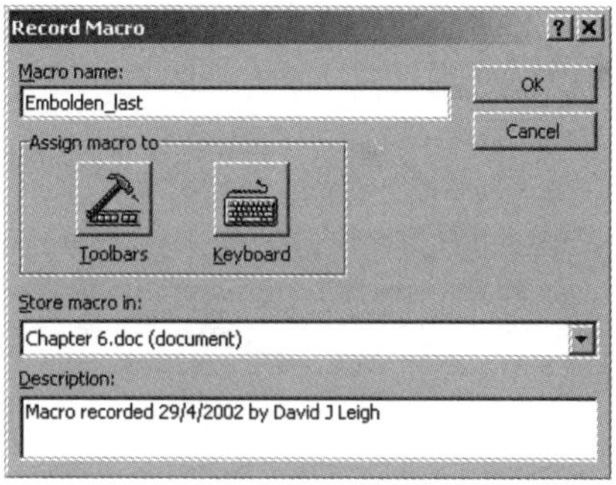

Figure 7.10 Word macro recording

Figure 7.11 Recording menu

The methods generated may be inspected from the *Macros* command, also called using *Alt-F8*. Choosing the *Edit* button will open the macro code file, shown in Figure 7.12. Four methods have been recorded, corresponding to moving left by one word, selecting the following word (highlighted by Word), changing it to bold style, and returning to the starting place by moving right by one word.

```
Sub Embolden_last()
'
'      Embolden_last Macro
'      Macro recorded 29/4/2002 by David J Leigh
'
      Selection.MoveLeft Unit:=wdWord, Count:=1
      Selection.MoveRight Unit:=wdWord, Count:=1, _
                          Extend:=wdExtend
      Selection.Font.Bold = wdToggle
      Selection.MoveRight Unit:=wdWord, Count:=1
End Sub
```

Figure 7.12 Word macro

CRUCIAL ACTIVITY

Record a macro in Word. Attach a shortcut key to it. Identify the program code generated corresponding to the macro.

There are two aspects of coding demonstrated in this example. For the first, the use of the dot notation is demonstrated in the example. Also shown is the way in which overlength lines may be dealt with. If the number of characters for a given statement is too long for the line in which the statement is placed, and it is important for formatting and documentation purposes to show all of the text, a continuation marker may be used. The line is broken at a convenient place, and an underscore character '_' is inserted.

An easy way to find other methods available like this is by experimenting. Recording a macro with different movements and actions leads to each one being shown in the corresponding code. From this, different facilities may easily be deduced. However, the details of all of the methods available are not discussed at length in this book, because they are specialised for use with Microsoft Word. If more information is needed, the *Help* facilities included with Word and with Visual Basic will assist in providing this.

Quick test

1. How are Visual Programming elements included in Microsoft Word documents?

2. What character is used for continuing long lines of Visual Basic coding?

Section 7

Visual components in Excel spreadsheets

In this section you will be introduced to Visual Basic methods associated with Microsoft Excel spreadsheets.

In the same way that Visual Basic code can be used to create particular effects in a Microsoft Word document, it can also be applied to Microsoft Excel spreadsheets. A small application has been given here as an example, to carry out a simple formatting operation. To make the user interface as friendly as possible, the formatting is associated with the active spreadsheet cell or cells, and is carried out using a button embedded in the spreadsheet.

The button is added to the spreadsheet using the Excel *Forms* toolbar. This is found in the *Toolbars* option of the *View* menu. The button control is chosen from the toolbar, and positioned on the spreadsheet in a convenient size, using the cross-hairs cursor provided. In the example shown in Figure 7.13 it has been located in cell *A1*, and sized to correspond to that cell.

Figure 7.13 Excel embedded button

During this positioning, the methods to be associated with the button may be added; or this may be carried out at a later stage. For the purposes of this example, the coding will be deferred. However, it is appropriate to associate a subroutine name with the button at this time, which can be done in the *Macro name* text box on the *Assign Macro* form. This form is displayed automatically during the positioning of the button, and closed with the *OK* option. The button should also be given a descriptive caption. The one chosen for the example is the same as the subroutine name, for consistency. It appears in Figure 7.13 as *Emphasise*.

If it later becomes necessary to alter any of the visual aspects of the command button, right-clicking it shows a menu with a number of options to help with such an alteration. For example, the name can easily be changed, or the text presented in a different font.

The method associated with the button is shown in Figure 7.14. It is added to the associated subroutine using the Visual Basic editor, found in the *Macro* option of the *Tools* menu. This will automatically open in the correct subroutine template of the selected item, which in this case is the ***Emphasise*** button. The method shown formats the currently active spreadsheet cell changing the typeface to bold and increasing the type size by two points. The opportunity has also been taken to introduce a further Visual Programming technique. In the program code the characteristics of the cells affected are `Font.Size` and `Font.Bold`, specifically those associated with the current `Selection`. These could have been named in full, but as they have common characteristics the `With` keyword has been used.

```
Sub Emphasise()
'
'   Emphasise current cell
'
       With Selection.Font
              .Size = .Size + 2
              .Bold = True
       End With
End Sub
```

Figure 7.14 Excel macro

CRUCIAL ACTIVITY

Record a macro in Excel. Attach a shortcut key to it. Add a suitable Visual Programming interface. Identify the program code generated corresponding to the macro.

This forms a programming block starting with `With` and finishing with `End With`. Inside this block, each partial name (for example, `.Bold`) is qualified with the parameter given to the `With` block, which in this example is `Selection.Font`. This has the effect of completing the partial name using the parameter, so that it has (in this case) the fully-qualified name `Selection.Font.Bold`. This enables a consistent approach to be taken to a number of parallel characteristics associated with a given control, data structure, or similar construction. It is another example of a robust programming approach, less liable to give rise to errors.

The effect of executing this code is shown in Figure 7.15. The three cells at the head of the lists have been selected, and the *Emphasise* button has been clicked. Only the selected cell(s) have been affected, and the change in size and presentation can readily be seen.

	A	B	C	D
1	Emphasise	**Name**	**Place**	**Code**
2		Colin	Lancs	2UT
3		Gill	Staffs	3BB
4		Jeff	Aston	7HD
5		John	Berks	2HE
6		Judith	Essex	8AP
7		Mary	Hunts	8RP
8		Mike	London	0HP
9		Tony	Wales	5SH

Figure 7.15 Use of command button

The same comments apply to this aspect of Visual Programming as in the previous section. Experimentation will help in learning how to include suitable methods in spreadsheet calculations. Inspection of macro-generated code will also help. There are specialised books which deal with spreadsheet coding, as well as sites on the World-Wide Web.

Quick test

1. How are controls added to a spreadsheet?
2. How are methods associated with controls in a spreadsheet?

Section 8

End of chapter assessment

Questions

1. In what ways does a Message Box help communication with the user of a Visual Program?
2. How does a subroutine differ from a function?
3. How may Visual Programs be easily embedded in World-Wide Web pages?
4. What is the `Select Case` statement used for?
5. What form of variable may be input using an `Inputbox`?
6. What is an easy way of specifying Visual Program code to be executed in a Microsoft Word or Excel application?

Answers

1. It is self-contained, and will therefore not interfere with other parts of the Visual Program. The execution of the Visual Program will not normally be resumed until the message is explicitly acknowledged. It is simple to specify, and is therefore less likely to cause errors.
2. They are both self-contained sequences of program code; but a function returns a value and a subroutine does not. Strictly, also, a function should have no effect on any non-local variable, existing precisely to calculate a value to be returned to the place from where it was called.
3. By the use of VBScript. This allows a Visual Program written in a 'cut down' version of Visual Basic to be executed from within the HTML script which defines the World-Wide Web page.
4. The `Select Case` statement is used to select from a number of possible outcomes which depend on the value of a variable or expression.
5. The type of variable returned by `Inputbox` is a text string. If any other interpretation is needed, it must be converted explicitly.
6. Constructing a macro to carry out the required actions, and then associating the corresponding Visual Program code with a suitable control in the application may most easily do this.

Section 9

Further reading and research

http://www.vb-bookmark.com/vbScript.html is a source of information about VBScript in general.

Chapter 8
Vision controls and other features

Chapter summary

This chapter opens with the introduction of controls which deal with graphics or pictures. Their characteristics and uses are demonstrated. These are extended with the description and demonstration of control visibility and enabling, which allow more precise management to be exercised over Visual Programs. Applications using lists of items are then shown.

Learning outcomes

The learning outcomes for this chapter are based around graphic and list controls, and the enabling of all controls. When you have successfully completed the chapter, you will be able to:

Outcome 1:   Implement Visual Programs using controls for holding images and other graphics.

Outcome 2:   Show only those controls which are available at a given time.

Outcome 3:   Use controls holding lists of items for selection and choice.

How will you be assessed on this?

Typically you may be asked to write Visual Programs which include images, which alter the display and availability characteristics of the controls and which deal with lists of items in different ways. These will be assessed by the production of working Visual Programs, and descriptions of the work you have carried out.

Section 1

Using the image control

You will learn about a simple control used to hold a graphic image.

It is useful to present certain information in a graphic form. Because of this, graphic controls may easily be included in a Visual Program. The most common of these are **images** and **picture boxes**. As their names imply, the latter is capable of holding a picture, and the former is a picture itself. Either of these may be used to hold a simple illustration.

The image control should be used if no more graphic functionality is needed than to provide an illustration. This will make the Visual Program smaller and more responsive. The image should be positioned in its container (for example, its form control) and sized appropriately. The selected image can then be added to the control, using its *Picture* property. Clicking on the *Picture* entry in the *Properties* window displays a standard window to retrieve an existing file, similar to that used when an existing document is opened. The required image can then be selected.

CRUCIAL TIP

There are many standard pictures stored in the Visual Basic system. They are typically found in the folders included in the `\Microsoft Visual Studio\Common\Graphics` pathway.

Any graphic item displayed using an image control will normally change the size of that control automatically to correspond to the graphic. This may be changed, if appropriate, but it is necessary to make sure that the *Stretch* property of the image control is set to *True* so that this may be carried out.

The picture shown by an image control is often in the form of an **icon**. This is a small file, typically no larger than 32×32 pixels in size. It is frequently used in a Windows environment to identify the type of a file, but is not limited to that. The Visual Programming environment supplies a number of these in addition to those which already form part of the operating system files. The pathways to these icons are usually found in the `\Icons` folder contained in the folder described in the Crucial tip above.

There is one familiar aspect of the image control which is frequently used – it has an associated *Click* method. It can therefore be used in the same way as a command button control. This is demonstrated with an example to show how the picture associated with the image control can be changed while the Visual Program is being executed.

The code for the *Click* method shown in Figure 8.1 is activated by the *Click* event associated with the image control `imgMoon` – in other words, when the mouse points at the image, and it is clicked. This executes the code shown, finishing with the `LoadPicture` method, which is the way in which the contents of an image are changed dynamically. This method takes the filename of a picture file (`Moon05.ico` in this example), and produces a result which can be loaded into the *Picture* property of the image control. The remainder of the code updates the filename, which is displayed to show which icon is currently on view.

```
Private Sub imgMoon_Click()
Dim sFilename, sFullMoon As String
'
'    Change icon displayed
'
        sFullMoon = "Moon05.ico"
        sFilename = "C:\Program Files" & _
                        "\Microsoft Visual Studio" & _
                        "\Common\Graphics " & _
                        " \Icons\Elements\" & sFullMoon
        imgMoon.Picture = LoadPicture(sFilename)
        lblFileName.Caption = "File name: " & sFullMoon

End Sub
```

Figure 8.1 Moon button

The original (static) value of this *Picture* property was set to refer to a similar icon, but with filename `Moon01.ico`, and the original filename was displayed statically in the caption of the label. Clicking directly on the icon in the example program changes the new moon to full! The effect of this is shown in Figure 8.2. The continuation lines in Figure 8.1 are used only for formatting purposes. The string variables `sFullMoon` and `sFilename` are used to help during program testing, and it is worth noting that intermediate values used in this way can be very helpful during debugging.

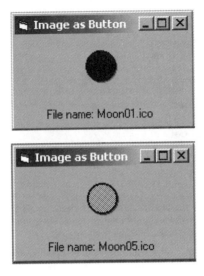

Figure 8.2 Before and after …

─── CRUCIAL ACTIVITY ───

Set up a form with an image whose *Picture* property is initialised as a suitable icon. Add code similar to that shown in Figure 8.1 to change the icon. Test the result of this Visual Program.

Quick test

1. Why should an image control be preferred to a picture box control?

2. What is an icon?

Section 2

Simple use of the picture box control

You will learn about other graphic image applications.

The image control is useful if the graphics have straightforward functionality. If more advanced work needs to be done, it is appropriate to use a picture box control. As well as holding an image, a picture box can also act as a **container** for other controls, in the same way that a form can contain other controls. A comparison of the property windows of image and picture box controls will show the added functionality of the latter, and their common properties.

─── CRUCIAL ACTIVITY ───

Make a list of the common properties of image and picture box controls, and the extra ones available to each.

As an example of the container capability shown by a picture box, the example above will be extended a little. A form is set up with two controls: a picture box and an image. The image used is Moon01.ico from the previous section, and picture box is sized to fit the icon, as shown in Figure 8.3. The height of the picture box is enough to contain the icon, which has a height of 480 twips. The length is calculated to hold eight similar icons, which have a width of 480 twips, with a space between each one.

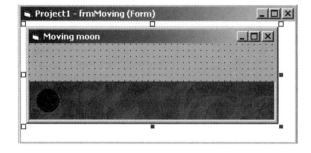

Figure 8.3 A picture box as a container

In this case, to ensure that the picture box is laid out in the containing form as shown, its *Align* property is set to 2 (*Align Bottom*). This causes it to be placed precisely at the bottom of the form without the need for any further calculation.

The intention is to use similar code to that of the previous section, but that each click on the icon will cause it to change to the next phase of the moon, and move towards the right as it does so. The icon library holds eight such images, which is why that number has been chosen. The code is shown in Figure 8.4.

```
Private Sub imgMoon_Click()
Static iCase As Integer
Dim sFilename As String
'
'   Select successive icons and display them and the corresponding filename
'
        iCase = iCase Mod 8
        iCase = iCase + 1
        sFilename = "C:\Program Files\Microsoft Visual Studio\Common\Graphics" & _
            "\Icons\Elements\Moon0" & Chr(iCase + Asc("0")) & ".ico"
    imgMoon.Picture = LoadPicture(sFilename)
    imgMoon.Left = iCase * 600 - 480
End Sub
```

Figure 8.4 Moving moon, with changing phases

The changes are kept in step by the variable iCase, which takes values from 1 to 8. Each time the subroutine is executed, its value is increased by 1, but if its value on entry is the maximum (8), it is returned to zero before the 1 is added to it. This is all managed automatically by the function Mod.

CRUCIAL TIP

Check that you know about the Mod function.

A special feature of the programming language is used in connection with this variable. Instead of it being declared with the keyword Dim, the keyword Static is used. The reason is that if Dim is used, the variable iCase would be set up dynamically in a fresh form each time the subroutine was executed; and erased afterwards. Because of this, iCase would not be able to hold a value at other times, when other parts of the Visual Program were being used. The keyword Static used in place of Dim makes sure that the same storage is used every time for the variable, so that it preserves its value at all times.

CRUCIAL CONCEPT

Some variables need to preserve their values, and require special treatment. Most do not, and are allocated dynamically. This provides for more efficient implementation.

The filename for the icon is constructed by concatenating its fixed parts with a single variable character. The function Chr takes a number formed from the offset from character '0' and the variable iCase and converts it into a character in the range '1' to '8'. The Asc function delivers the correct base value corresponding to the character '0'. The movement is managed by changing the *Left* property of the icon: a move of 600 twips to the right in each case.

One cosmetic use has been made of the capabilities of the picture box. Because, as a graphic control it can hold a picture, a background graphic has been included using its Picture property. This is intended to represent a relatively stormy night sky; but loses some of its verisimilitude because the figure is reproduced in grayscale only.

Quick test

1. What is the most obvious error which occurs while the above example Visual Program is being executed?

2. Why are measurements given in twips?

Visible and invisible controls

You will learn about one way of enabling and disabling controls.

The same apparent functionality of the previous example will be revisited in this section, but approached in a different way. It will make use of another property of controls, whether they are *Visible* (or not). This means that while a Visual Program is being executed, there may be controls present which cannot be seen. This can be particularly useful when including program code which may only be used under certain circumstances, and the associated control can be seen by the user.

Each of the icons used is put into its own image control. These are organised in a control array for simplicity, as will be apparent from the program code. The design view of the Visual Program is shown in Figure 8.5; it is important that not all of the icons will be visible at the same time while the Visual Program is being executed.

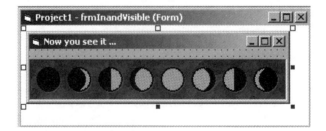

Figure 8.5 Using the *Visible* property

The first requirement when the Visual Program starts execution is to make all of the images invisible except the first. This could be done in the design view, but has here been done dynamically. This is carried out using one of the methods which is present in every Visual Program, and is associated with the form control. This is Form_Load, and is executed as any form is being loaded. It is therefore a convenient subroutine to store program code which is to initialise variables and controls within the Visual Program. In this case, the first icon is made visible (whether it was originally or not), and the others are all made invisible. That is, the *Visible* property is set to *False* in each instance. This is illustrated in the first part of Figure 8.6. Notice the use of the For/Next keywords to construct a counting loop.

```
Private Sub Form_Load()

'
'    Make image 1 visible, images 2 - 8 invisible
'
Dim iMoon As Integer

        imgMoon(0).Visible = True
        For iMoon = 1 To 7
                imgMoon(iMoon).Visible = False
        Next iMoon

End Sub
'==========================================================
Private Sub imgMoon_Click(Index As Integer)
'
'    Make this moon invisible, and make the next one visible
'

        imgMoon(Index).Visible = False
        imgMoon((Index + 1) Mod 8).Visible = True

End Sub
```

Figure 8.6 Moving moon, with changing phases – alternative approach

CRUCIAL ACTIVITY

Look up the For/Next keywords in the Visual Basic Help files. Make suitable notes as reminders.

Now it is sufficient that, when any image is clicked, it should make itself invisible, and its successor should be made visible. As only one image will be visible, and therefore accessible, at any one time, this will have the functionality desired. Once again the Mod function is used, this time in conjunction with the control array of images. This implies that the first image is the successor of the eighth image, as required. It works particularly well, and avoids the error of the previous section, because the indexes associated with arrays have lowest value zero.

Quick test

1. Is a control accessible when it is not visible?

2. What kind of variable is used to control a For/Next construction?

Section 4

Enabled and disabled controls

You will learn how to enable and how to disable controls.

The practice of hiding or otherwise disabling material which is not needed at a given point in an application has the general name of **information hiding**. This allows the user to concentrate only on those aspects of the system which are currently relevant. The ways in which controls may be hidden to assist in this process were introduced in the previous section.

It is, however, sometimes better to let controls which are not currently active to remain visible, as a reminder that they are present, but still to make sure that they cannot be used. This will be illustrated with command buttons, but used in a way similar to the previous example.

—————————— CRUCIAL CONCEPT ——————————

Information hiding is an important part of producing robust applications.

A control array of three command buttons is set up, with suitable captions. The example illustrated in Figure 8.7 shows this example while it is being executed. As may be seen, only one of the command buttons appears fully visible. The other two are arranged with their details 'greyed out': visible, but not accessible to the user.

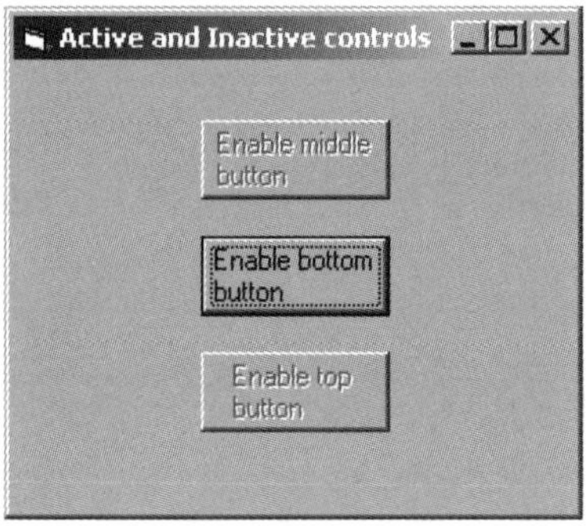

Figure 8.7 Enabling and disabling controls

The property used to create this effect is *Enable*. When this property is set to True, the control takes in its normal appearance; when it is *False*, the full visibility is reduced. This property should not be confused with the *Visible* property, which makes the control completely invisible when it is set to *False*.

The three command buttons are initialised in the display view of the Visual Program with their *Enable* properties set respectively, reading downwards, to *True*, *False*, *False*. (This does not correspond to Figure 8.7: that shows the form after the top command button has been pressed.) The program code is organised in the same way as the second part of Figure 8.6.

The property being changed is defined after the dot separator. Referring to Figure 8.8, note once again that the control name, being part of a control array, is given its index or subscript first, before the dot. In this example there are three members of the control array, so that the values 0, 1 and 2 are needed as successive subscripts to the members of the control array, which is again managed by the use of the Mod function.

```
Private Sub cmdEnable_Click(Index As Integer)
'
'    Disable this button, enable the next
'
        cmdEnable(Index).Enabled = False
        cmdEnable((Index + 1) Mod 3).Enabled = True

End Sub
```

Figure 8.8 Enabling and disabling command buttons

Quick test

1. In which order do the dot and the subscript appear in a reference to a member of a control array?

2. How does the Enable property differ from the Visible property?

Section 5

List box controls

You will learn about one way of dealing with lists of items.

The option button control was introduced in Chapter 5. It offers a way of selecting one from a number of mutually exclusive items. This approach can take up considerable space, however, when the number of options exceeds three. It can also be difficult for the user to comprehend when a large array of options is presented.

Figure 8.9 List box control

To avoid these difficulties, the **list box** control enables a choice to be made from a number of possibilities. Each is described by suitable text to allow the correct choice to be made. The list box can handle a large number of options, but not all may be visible. In Figure 8.9 there is room to display only five items from a longer list (which includes 11 items, but there is no way of deciding this from the list box display). If there is enough room, all possible items are shown; if not, a scroll bar is included to allow access to the other items. This is similar to the scroll bars available to the text box control described in Chapter 5. It differs, however, in that it is provided automatically when it is needed, and not otherwise. It is also a more generalised form of the drive list box and the directory list box controls introduced in Chapter 6.

The list can be set up in the design view of the list box. The *List* property allows successive data to be entered, with the entries separated by *Ctrl + Enter*. If a suitable list already exists, for example in a text file, it may be input while the Visual Program is being executed. This may conveniently be done in the Form_Load method, as described in Section 3 above. The elements are added to any existing list. An example of suitable code is given in Figure 8.10.

```
Private Sub Form_Load()
'
'    Load List Box
'
Dim sName As String

        Open ''I:\Names.txt'' For Input As #1
        While Not EOF(1)
                Input #1, sName
                lstNames.AddItem sName
        Wend
        Close #1

End Sub
```

Figure 8.10 Loading a list box

The items are read one at a time from the input file, in a similar way to that shown in Chapter 3, until the end of file is reached. As each one is input, it is added to the contents of the list box, using the AddItem method. The items are directed towards the list box using dot notation and the name of the list box – in this case lstNames.

The entries in the list are given in the order in which they are input. This is convenient when the data come from a well-defined source. It is sometimes more appropriate for them to appear in sorted order, however. This may be done by setting the *Sorted* property of the list box to *True*.

─── CRUCIAL ACTIVITY ───

It is also possible to insert items at any point in the list in a list box. Look at the help file to discover how to do this.

Once the list box has been set up, it is used to select one from a fixed number of items. This may be done in several ways, but in each case the selected item is found in the Text element associated with the list box. This highlighted list member has not yet been accessed in Figure 8.9. The selection and highlighting can be carried out by a single click on the list element. Alternatively, successive elements can be highlighted using the up and down arrow navigation keys. This facility is built in to the functionality of the list box control.

The code to place the selected member on the form is given in the first subroutine shown in Figure 8.11, and is accessed when the event associated with the command button cmdSelectNow click occurs. This program code takes the selected item and places it in the caption field of a label control. This result is shown in Figure 8.12.

It is also customary to allow list box items to be chosen directly using a double click event. This can be done for the list box from the lstNames_DblClick event, and is demonstrated in the second subroutine in Figure 8.11.

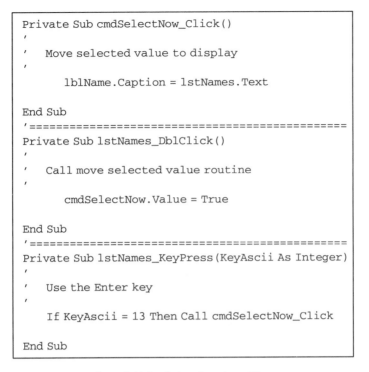

```
Private Sub cmdSelectNow_Click()
'
'    Move selected value to display
'
        lblName.Caption = lstNames.Text

End Sub
'================================================
Private Sub lstNames_DblClick()
'
'    Call move selected value routine
'
        cmdSelectNow.Value = True

End Sub
'================================================
Private Sub lstNames_KeyPress(KeyAscii As Integer)
'
'    Use the Enter key
'
        If KeyAscii = 13 Then Call cmdSelectNow_Click

End Sub
```

Figure 8.11 Retrieving the selected item

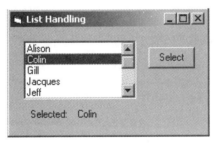

Figure 8.12 List item selected

Finally for this example it is possible to accept a highlighted element from a list box using interaction from the keyboard. The lstNames_KeyPress event occurs whenever a key is pressed during the selection process using the list box. Because it is customary to recognise this event formally from the user's point of view only when the *Enter* key is used, this has to be dealt with using a program selection statement.

The third subroutine shown in Figure 8.11 is entered when any key is pressed, but only the *Enter* key value calls the formal selection from the list box contents. The integer ASCII code corresponding to this key is 13, as shown in this subroutine, and also in one of the examples in Chapter 7.

It would have been possible in each of the other cases to duplicate the code shown in the first subroutine, which is not extensive. This is contrary to the guidelines for robust programming. If any changes to the display usage were made, it would then be possible to make them in one place and not in the others. Such inconsistencies may be avoided by calling the same code, which would then only need amendment (if appropriate) in a single program code location.

CRUCIAL CONCEPT

Do not duplicate program code intended for identical functions.

It is reasonable and quite valid to call the first subroutine directly from one of the others. This uses the statement `Call cmdSelectNow_Click`, as in the third subroutine. An alternative approach has been chosen in the second subroutine, to illustrate another possibility. The selection is designed to take place when the command button is clicked. This event can be simulated from within the program code by setting the *Value* property of the `cmdSelectNow` button to `True`, as shown.

Quick test

1. Is a command button required to select from a list box?
2. What are the two ways of loading a list box?

Section 6

Combo box controls

You will learn about an alternative way of dealing with a list of items.

There is an alternative way of accessing a list of items: by the use of a **combo box** control. This is similar in appearance to a list box, but differs in some of the details. As suggested by its name, it has a combination of attributes: it combines some of the functionality of a list box with that of a text box. It enables a user to suggest some characteristics of the list item required, or even to propose an element not found in a list of suggestions.

The examples used in the preceding section all apply to the combo box. Each of the code examples can be safely copied, with only those program code amendments needed to recognise that the combo box control is being used, rather than the list box.

CRUCIAL ACTIVITY

Copy the examples of Section 5. Change the list box to a combo box, and make the necessary program code amendments. Check that your changes work.

There are two changes that should be recognised in this alternative approach. The first is largely cosmetic, but may be important in some users' applications. The combo box appears in its container as a single line only, which is useful if there is limited space available. The full list of recognised elements is made available using the drop down button at the right of the combo box.

The second allows direct user input, and is demonstrated in Figure 8.13, where an entry not found in the associated list has been added. This has also been selected, as shown in the display in the label control at the bottom of the form.

There are three possible appearances of the combo box, determined by the *Style* property. The default, shown above, is *0 – Dropdown Combo*. The second, *1 – Simple Combo*, uses a single line only, without the drop down button. The list items are accessed using the arrow keys, or the user may enter any requirement directly. This corresponds to the text box appearance of the combo box. The final appearance is *2 – Dropdown List*. This is similar in appearance to that shown in Figure 8.13. The difference is that it does not allow user-defined insertions: the item chosen must come from the list.

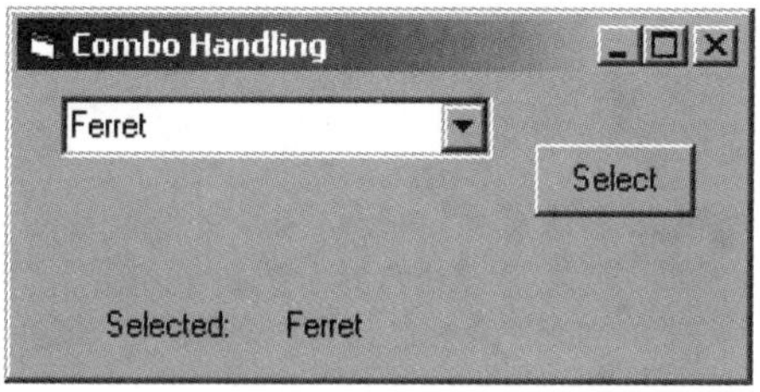

Figure 8.13 Combo box control

When constructing lists in either list boxes or combo boxes during the execution of a Visual Program, it is sometimes necessary to clear the whole list or to remove items. The list can be emptied using the `Clear` method; this is qualified in the usual way, and an example might thus appear as cboNames.Clear, making the corresponding list ready to receive new entries.

To remove an item, the `RemoveItem` method is used. This takes a single argument, which is the index of the item to be removed. This means that such an index value must be able to be deduced or calculated before the corresponding item can be removed. If the item to be removed is known only by its value, rather than by its index, then the list must be searched for the item, keeping track of the corresponding index.

A suggested approach is shown in Figure 8.14. The value of the `ListCount` associated with the list box gives the total number of entries. The first has an index of 0, and the last a value of `ListCount – 1`. If the required value is found, the item with the corresponding index may then be removed.

```
For iIndex = 0 To lstNames.ListCount - 1
    If lstNames.List(iIndex) = sValue Then
        lstNames.RemoveItem iIndex
    End If
Next iIndex
```

Figure 8.14 Removing an item from a list

The algorithm described in Figure 8.14 is not efficient for a large list, because every item is inspected in every case. A more efficient way of finding a corresponding item may be developed if the list is in order. The value of the *Sorted* property of the list box or combo box control should be saved beforehand, and restored afterwards. If a list value greater than the search item is found, the search may be terminated. For even more efficiency, a 'binary chop' search algorithm could be used.

--- CRUCIAL TIP ---

It is often worth looking for more efficient ways of carrying out list searches. But unless the list is very large, the gain in efficiency is unlikely to outweigh the loss in simplicity and associated robustness.

To finish off, two quick and simple questions to help to decide whether to use a list box or a combo box for a given application.

- How much room is there on the form?
    - If there is not much room, use a combo box, because it only takes a single line. (Remember, however, that it has a drop down effect when used.)

- Do you want the user to be limited to the list items, or to add an option if necessary?
  - If the user may add options, a combo box must be used. If the list is fixed, use a list box or a combo box with its *Style* property set to *2*.

Quick test

1. What different kinds of combo boxes are available to a Visual Program?

2. What two controls are combined in a combo box control?

End of chapter assessment

Questions

1. How is a suitable graphic associated with an image control?
2. What is the difference between a variable declared with the keyword `Static` and one declared with the keyword `Dim`?
3. When does the `Form_Load` event occur?
4. Why is information hiding important?
5. How many times should common program code be written for a particular application?
6. What methods are associated with list boxes and combo boxes?

Answers

1. This may be done at design time, using its *Picture* property. Alternatively, it may be done while the Visual Program is being executed, using the `LoadPicture` method. In each case, the graphic file to be used must be specified by name.

2. Statically-declared variables exist for the whole of the execution time of a Visual Program. Non-statically-declared variables exist only during the time their containing subroutine is being executed, and are destroyed after each time the subroutine finishes execution.

3. The `Form_Load` event occurs each time a given form is loaded. It is therefore useful to initialise variables using the `Form_Load` event associated with the main form of a Visual Program.

4. To allow Visual Programs to be as robust as possible, only as much information should be present at a given time and in a given routine as will be needed then and there. This means that unwanted side effects may be minimised, so that errors are less likely to be generated.

5. Any common code should be written only once, and may conveniently be held in a subroutine. It should then be referenced by calling the subroutine. This avoids any difficulties associated with updating the code if there is any need to do so, because it needs to be done only once, and in one place.

6. These include, among others, `AddItem`, `Clear`, `Refresh`, `RemoveItem` and `SetFocus`. (Make sure that you know the difference between a **property** and a **method**.)

Section 8

Further reading and research

There are many examples in *http://www.vb-helper.com/howto.htm* of different complexities. Start with the easier ones.

Chapter 9
Extending Visual Program facilities

Chapter summary

The chapter opens with the use of more than one form in a Visual Program, and the organisation of several forms. The addition of program code modules for common routines is followed by their application to simple error handling. Consideration of the use of the mouse interface is introduced by a reminder about the WIMP interface. The final section deals with simple storyboarding for design purposes.

Learning outcomes

This chapter introduces learning outcomes for extending the facilities available to a Visual Program. When you have been successful in completing this chapter, you will be able to:

Outcome 1: **Use more than one form for each application.**
Outcome 2: **Construct visual print applications.**
Outcome 3: **Organise multiple forms for the best effect.**
Outcome 4: **Apply modules used for code only.**
Outcome 5: **Use simple error processing.**
Outcome 6: **Detect and use information made available by the mouse interface.**
Outcome 7: **Use the storyboard approach to designing larger event-driven programs.**

How will you be assessed on this?

Typically you may be asked to write Visual Programs using multiple forms which are used for different purposes and to demonstrate different ways of using the mouse. You may also have to answer questions about the use of independent modules for common program code, about error handling and about the design of event-driven and Visual Programs.

Section 1

Multiple forms

Some of the reasons for using more than one form in a single application are discussed.

It is possible to carry out many tasks using a single form. The form itself can be sized and moved around the screen to suit the needs of the application. Command buttons can be manoeuvred to parts of the form where they are wanted, made visible or enabled as required. Colours, backgrounds and other properties and controls can be defined to correspond to each part of the process being executed. This leads, however, to considerable complication. It can be done, but there are better ways. Referring back to

Occam's razor in Chapter 7, it is also recommended that *KISS* ('Keep it simple ...') is a good idea.

Following on from this, it is a good idea if each task has a single corresponding form. The controls set in this form will not be moved unless there is a specific reason to do so. This implies that the design view will be the same as the appearance while the Visual Program is being executed. The exception to this will only occur when controls are rendered invisible for a specific reason.

As a simple example, consider how an exchange can be arranged between two forms. The default form for the project is used, and a further form is inserted into the application using the *Add Form* option from the *Project* menu. The two forms are named `frmFirst` and `frmSecond` respectively. The three event subroutines are then set up as shown in Figure 9.1.

`Private Sub Form_Load()`
`    frmSecond.Left = Left`
`    frmSecond.Top = Top`
`End Sub`
`' =====================`
`Private Sub Form_Click()`
`    frmSecond.Visible = True`
`    Visible = False`
`End Sub`
	`Private Sub Form_Click()`
	`    frmFirst.Visible = True`
	`    Visible = False`
	`End Sub`

Program code for frmFirst	Program code for frmSecond

Figure 9.1 Form exchange

When the original form is loaded, the first event subroutine on the left of Figure 9.1 is executed, which makes sure that the two forms occupy the same place. `frmSecond` in not visible initially, and has not yet been made visible, but it is still possible to set up its properties. When `frmFirst` is clicked, the second subroutine on the left of Figure 9.1 is executed. This causes `frmSecond` to be set visible, and the current form, `frmFirst`, to be set non-visible. A similar click on `frmSecond` reverses the process.

Any controls contained by the two forms are made visible or non-visible with their parent form. This allows the principles of encapsulation and information hiding to be enabled with no further effort on the part of the implementor. This approach to straightforward enabling of good design principles is common in Visual Programming. Even so, it should always be checked if there is any doubt. For example, if a control should be disabled at any time, it is safer to ensure that this happens by disabling it while the Visual Program is being executed, even though it has been disabled at design time. In this way, if its containing control is reinitialised, the state of any of its previous properties can be made certain. This may take up a few instructions, but that is far better than implementing an application incorrectly.

──────────────── CRUCIAL TIP ────────────────
Take a little longer to be sure, even if it needs a little more work. There is **no** substitute for accuracy.

One reason for using a second form has to do with the printing of output. A printer may be considered as a simple output device, and text may be prepared for it directly. The method used, unsurprisingly, is `Print`. As usual, it should be qualified to show that the output is to be directed to the printer. This is illustrated in Figure 9.2. A simple calculation is carried out, and the data are printed out for wider display. Because all activities depend on events, this has been enabled when the application's form is clicked.

```
Private Sub Form_Click()
Dim iLength, iBreadth as Integer
Dim sTitle as String

        sTitle = "Calculating the area of a rectangle"
        iLength = 5: iBreadth = 4
        Printer.Print sTitle
        Printer.Print "Length is"; iLength;
        Printer.Print "Breadth is"; iBreadth
        Printer.Print "Area is"; iLength * iBreadth

End Sub
```

Figure 9.2 Output to printer

Some aspects specific to the `Print` method have been shown in this example. Strings and numbers can be output directly, and may come from variables, formulae or constant values. The default is that a newline follows each item output. This may be overridden by following the values to be output with a semicolon ';', which suppresses the newline.

There is, however, a simple but powerful method available which enables an entire container control to be printed. This is `PrintForm`, which transfers the entire visible contents of the form or picture box to whichever destination is specified. This is typically the default printer. In this way, an entire page may be set up for printing. It may then be checked, before being sent to that printer. If it is not yet acceptable for printing, it may be respecified using the Visual Program which generates it. It need be printed only when it has been confirmed to be satisfactory.

───────── CRUCIAL CONCEPT ─────────

Because this is a Visual Program, based on the appearance of any item on the screen, default printing is usually limited in definition. This means that full advantage may not be taken of the accuracy of a high-definition printer.

There is one further aspect to be verified. The text and images printed using this method depend on the *AutoRedraw* property of the form or picture box used as the container. This must be set to *True*. If not, only those items or parts of items currently shown on the screen will be printed. An example of the use of this method will be developed in the next section.

───────── CRUCIAL ACTIVITY ─────────

Design a letter layout, including graphics. Check its content and layout. Use `PrintForm` to print a copy.

Quick test

1. How is a newline specified when printing text?

2. What are the advantages of using more than one form in a Visual Program?

Section 2

Child forms in an MDI form

In this section you will be introduced to a way of organising two or more forms in a single application.

One way of organising and moving between forms has been described above. Another possibility is given by the use of the **Multiple Document Interface** form, more commonly referred to as the **MDI** form. This is a container for forms, in the same way that a form or a picture box can be a container for other controls. It allows a form to be usefully constructed whose size exceeds the window size available.

The use of a form acting as a container has already been used explicitly in several places. It was introduced in Chapter 2 as a receiver for text generated by a Visual Program. Its use as a blank form for writing on, therefore, is familiar. But because it can also contain other visible items, it can be more flexibly applied. A simple extension would be the use of a pre-prepared graphic or logo. It can therefore, quite simply, be used to format suitably designed notepaper.

CRUCIAL CONCEPT
Visual applications are not limited to displays on screens.

A Visual Program may contain only a single MDI form, but that MDI form can hold many other forms. The MDI form is known as the parent, and the other forms are its child forms. Forms may also be used outside the MDI parent, so that they are not its children. To distinguish the two categories, those which are child forms have their *MDIChild* property set to *True*. For the others, it is set to *False*.

This approach offers a way to organise forms in a single Visual Program, particularly if one or more are larger than the screen size available. If a child form is larger than its MDI parent, scroll bars are automatically added to that parent. All parts of the large child form may then be inspected in turn, using the scroll bars.

To initialise a project using this facility, first open as usual with a form. Then use the *Project* menu option *Add MDI form*. Add a further form from the same menu, and set the *MDIChild* property of each to *True*. This has been done in the Visual Program shown in Figure 9.3. The first form has been given the caption *Net for a cube*; the second has *Print ?*.

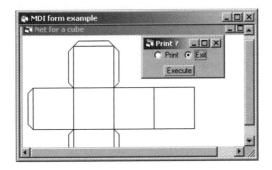

Figure 9.3 MDI form use

The second form is used as a container for controls dealing with printing of the contents of the first form. It will not interfere with the printing of the first form. Although it appears to be on top of it, it remains logically separate. An alternative to a two-button interface has been chosen for illustrative purposes only. The position of the scroll bars and the two forms shows how these bars may be used to access different parts of the forms automatically.

CRUCIAL ACTIVITY

Make up a suitable test program to contain an MDI form and a child form. The child form should have graphic or text content inserted both at design time and while the Visual Program is being executed. Use the scroll bars to ensure that all parts of the child form are accessible. Now try the same exercise with the *AutoRedraw* property of the child form set to *False*. Make a note of the differences you see.

The positioning of the code to activate the two forms is important. Because of the layout, the second form should be activated after the first form. If these operations are not carried out in this order, the first form will become visible on top of the second, thus blanking it out. The forms should therefore be explicitly made visible in the appropriate order.

```
Private Sub MDIForm_Load
'
'Set up forms in order
'
    frmCube.Visible = True
    frmPrint.Top = 350
    frmPrint.Left = 2880
    frmPrint.Height = 1000
    frmPrint.Width = 2000
    frmPrint.Visible = True
End Sub
```

Figure 9.4 Multiple form initialisation

This is illustrated in Figure 9.4. At the same time, the second form has been positioned and sized explicitly. While this is not essential, it demonstrates that the Visual Program may take absolute control of its layout as it is being initialised. This has used the Load subroutine of the master control, which is now the MDI form.

CRUCIAL TIP

Make decisions about the appearance of your Visual Program interface and ensure that what you decide is carried out. In some instances, dynamic setting while the Visual Program is being executed is safer because it can be explicitly debugged, with critical values checked in the development environment.

This is an illustrative example only. It has many deficiencies. One of the most obvious is shown during execution if the first form is clicked. The second form disappears, because the first form has become active, and is shown in preference to the second form. This is simple to correct in this case. If the first form cannot be acted upon by a click, then it cannot obscure the second form. This can be done by setting its *Enable* property to *False*. This will only work on the assumption that it will then form a static display, requiring no further changes.

Quick test

1. What might be the use of a form which is not fully visible?

2. What special operations must be carried out to provide an MDI form with scroll bars?

Section 3

Modules for code only

While introducing a container for independent subroutines and functions, some aspects of error handling are visited.

Some subroutines carry out common calculations. These calculations have enough in common that they are best implemented only once, and called from whichever parts of the application need them. Such calculations are best organised as subroutines or functions. These are then stored in the Visual Program and used when they are needed.

However, the subroutines so far demonstrated are all based on events connected with the controls used for Visual Programs. It is not sensible to start adding subroutines to controls which may be used by other controls. If a sequence of program code is to be shared between controls, it should be independent of the specific characteristics of those controls. Otherwise, it would be too difficult to organise the sharing of the common routine.

Therefore the subroutines to be developed for these purposes should be stored independently. They should be placed in storage organised for that purpose. This facility is provided within independent code modules, which act as containers for independent subroutines and functions. These are easily added to Visual Programs, and then form part of their functionality.

To illustrate this approach, the editor program introduced in Chapter 3 will again be used. The part of the editor considered involves the opening of files. This activity can lead to a number of errors, but some are more common than others. The most common error is the incorrect specification of a file name. It may be due to attempting to read from a non-existent file, or to simple misspelling which may give rise to this. A routine to deal with such errors will be produced, and stored within an independent code module.

It is first necessary to add this code module to contain such a routine. This is done using the _Add Module_ option of the _Project_ menu. This forms a container for the independent subroutine code, in a similar way to that used for controls and their containers. It is then up to the programmer to specify the kind of subroutine to be used. In this case, the subroutine will be returning a value to its calling point, to indicate the success (or otherwise) of the operation. It is therefore a function, rather than a subroutine.

CRUCIAL CONCEPT

A **function** returns a value to its calling point. A **subroutine** only carries out particular activities.

This may be done by adding suitable text, starting with `Function` and the name of the subroutine. As is usual, the Development Environment is helpful during this activity. It adds identifying brackets for the parameters of the subroutine, which must be provided even if it uses no parameters. The `End Function` text is also added, implicitly defining the position to add the program code of the subroutine. Alternatively, the _Add Procedure_ option can be chosen from the _Tools_ menu.

This is shown in Figure 9.5, which demonstrates the attributes to be given to a subroutine. The functionality of the subroutine will determine its type and scope. Because this subroutine will be needed outside the code module, it must be given _Public_ scope. Because it will return a value, it must be of type _Function_.

The requirements to be carried out by the function are specified by its input and output, and any side effects which it is expected to perform. It needs to know whether a file is to be opened for reading or for writing. It needs to know what file name is to be used. It should check the filename for validity. It should then check whether the file exists or not, and take appropriate action. It should inform the calling point about the validity of the filename, and whether the action requested has been successful.

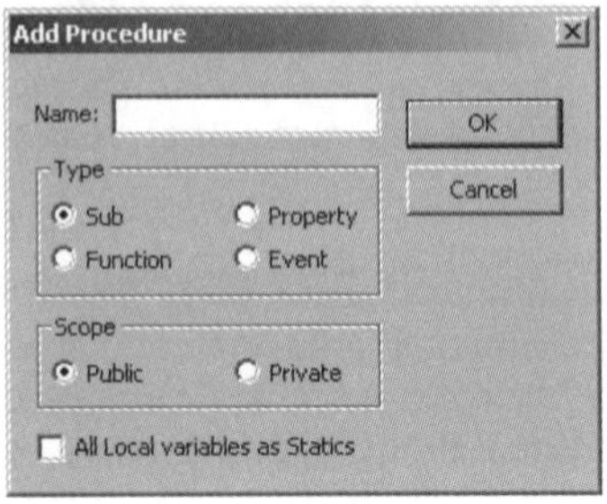

Figure 9.5 *Add Procedure* menu

CRUCIAL TIP

When a requirements analysis of this nature has taken place, it is essential to check the design against those requirements.

The pseudocode design for this function appears in Figure 9.6. This will not be encoded in complete detail, but certain aspects will be illustrated. Each return statement within the function ensures that no further program code within the function will be obeyed. It will therefore not be possible to attempt to open a file if the filename given is not valid. It will be understood, for this occasion, that the only operations expected are reading and writing. Therefore, if one of these is not specified, the other will be assumed. This is easily managed in this instance by the use of a Boolean parameter for this purpose.

```
If the file name is not valid
                               return-1
If the file is to be read and does not exist,
                               return-2
If the file is to be written and does exist,
                               return-3
Otherwise return 0
```

Figure 9.6 Function design

The corresponding program code outline is shown in Figure 9.7. There are some important items here which should be carefully noted.

```
Public Function                  Open sFileName For Input As #1
       funCheckFileName _        If bForReading Then
       (sFileName As String, _       If Err Then
       bForReading As Boolean)           funCheckFileName = -2
       As Integer                Else
Dim bFileNameOK As Boolean              Close #1
                                        funCheckFileName = 0
'  Insert code here to            End If
'  check file name               Else
   If Not bFileNameOK Then            If Err Then
       funCheckFileName = -1             funCheckFileName = 0
       Exit Function             Else
End If                                   Close #1
                                        funCheckFileName = -3
'  Turn off error trap                End If
'  for this routine only         End If
   On Error Resume Next
                                 End Function

Program code for function header | Program code for file check
```

Figure 9.7 Program code to check file

CRUCIAL ACTIVITY

Compare the contents of Figures 9.6 and 9.7. Make sure that you can see the corresponding items.

The first of these shows how a value is assigned to a function. A simple assignment statement is used to pass the required value to the function name. The second is the management of an early exit from the function. This is carried out by the `Exit Function` statement.

The statement `On Error Resume Next` deals with the actions taken in case there is an error in the Visual Program. It instructs the error-handling mechanisms to carry on with the next instruction after any error has been detected during the execution of the Visual Program. The implication of this is extremely important. It effectively disables any error trapping, which is a very serious step to take. As a safety precaution, then, its effects are kept local in action. Once the routine is left in which this statement has been executed, its effects are removed.

It is still possible to find out if any error has occurred. The `Err` object, automatically included in any Visual Program, has a value `True` if any fault has been detected. It may be checked at any time. In this example, an attempt is made to open the given file for reading. If the file name format has been properly checked for correctness, the only error likely will occur if no file of that name is present.

If a reading request has been made (`bForReading` has the value `True`), and it was not possible to open the file, the file does not exist. The appropriate function error code is therefore returned. Otherwise, success is signalled, and the file is closed. This is done so that there are no side effects as a result of this function being called, which is highly desirable from a Software Engineering point of view. A similar approach is taken for the request to write to a file, taking regard of the design requirements given in Figure 9.6.

Quick test

1. Which is preferable: `If bForReading Then` or `If bForReading = True Then`?

2. Where are independent functions and subroutines stored in a Visual Program?

Section 4

Mouse cursors and operations

You will learn about some details of mouse events and presentation.

The user interface available to a Visual Program is known as **WIMP**, from the initials of its components: window, icon, mouse, pull-down menu. The first two of those have been introduced, and the last one is not within the scope of this book in any but its most primitive form. Many of the mouse operations have been accepted implicitly when used with the controls so far described. There are a number of explicit events connected with mouse operations which will be introduced in this section. The appearance of the mouse pointer will also be explored.

CRUCIAL ACTIVITY

There are good descriptions of the **menu** control in the help files. Look at them now so that you know where to look when you need them.

Each control typically has three mouse events associated with it. These are MouseDown, MouseUp and MouseMove. The first two are called when a mouse button is clicked or released. The information available at this time includes which mouse button was clicked, whether any special keys were pressed on the keyboard, and the coordinates of the mouse pointer within the control.

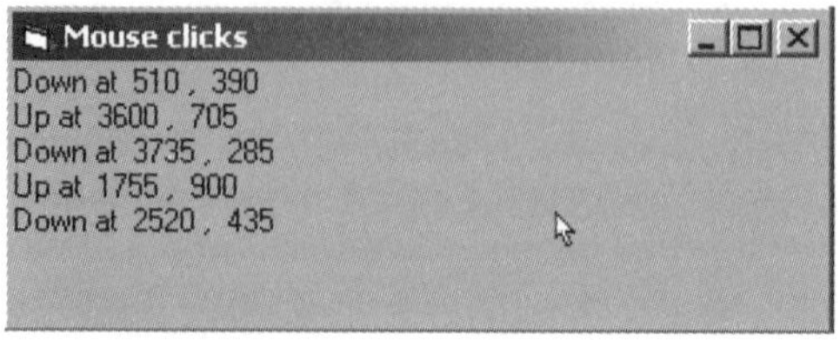

Figure 9.8 MouseDown and MouseUp

A simple example of this is shown in Figure 9.8. The program code consists of a single Print method for each of the MouseDown and MouseUp events. The code for the first of these is

```
Print "Down at "; X; ", "; Y
```

The second is similar. The coordinates given show that the mouse has been moved between the MouseDown and MouseUp events, and that the last MouseUp event has not yet taken place.

Figure 9.9 MouseMove

The MouseMove event is similar, and is illustrated in Figure 9.9 using the code fragment

```
Cls:
Print "Mouse pointer is at"; X; ", "; Y
```

which uses the Cls method introduced in Chapter 5. The MouseMove event is called whenever the mouse pointer moves relative to the relevant control. In this case, it clears the control and then displays its present coordinates. As the mouse is moved around the form, the figures representing its position are updated. Because the form is cleared at each event, owing to the speed of the system, only the coordinate figures appear to change. In the example, the mouse pointer is centred on the 'o' of 'Mouse', whose coordinates are (180, 105).

──────── CRUCIAL CONCEPT ────────

The MouseMove event occurs **every** time the mouse is moved. This can happen a large number of times while a mouse is being positioned. This leads to the event handler being called **every** time a move, however small, is sensed.

Another familiar aspect of working with a mouse is the appearance of its pointer. This may be shown in one of many formats, according to the application which is running. This appearance is implemented with reference to the control to which the mouse is pointing. This is realised by the *MousePointer* property. A number of possibilities are presented using a drop-down menu when an application is being constructed for its initial appearance.

The property is actually an integer value, and this can be changed during the execution of the Visual Program. A typical example of this occurs when an activity is taking place which leads to the movement or resizing of a window. The usual way of signalling this is to change the cursor's appearance into a pair or a set of arrows. This would be done by changing the *MousePointer* property value to a number in the range 5–9.

CRUCIAL TIP

Don't forget to save the value corresponding to the original appearance, so that the appearance can be reset afterwards.

An example suggesting when it would be a good idea to change the appearance of the mouse pointer is found in the text editor introduced in Chapter 3. The file handling associated with the reading of a large file can take several seconds if the file is large. So that the user is not left without visual clues, it is good practice to display information that the Visual Program is behaving as it is meant to. This is typically done by changing the appearance to an hourglass, signifying the passage of time.

This would involve the declaration of a new variable in the `cmdLoad_Click` subroutine shown in Figure 3.6. This receives the current value of `frmEditor.MousePointer` at the beginning of the subroutine, which is then set to 11. The saved value is used to restore the original cursor at the end of the routine.

CRUCIAL ACTIVITY

Make the modification. Check the behaviour of the modified Visual Program.

If the cursors provided by the Visual Programming development environment do not correspond to the requirements of the application, more can be found in different locations within the computer system. Chapter 8 has introduced libraries of icons. Cursors are found in similar locations, but are also available directly in standard operating system files. Any reasonably sized bitmap may be used, but normally only those with extensions `.CUR` or `.ICO` are used.

Quick test

1. What happens if mouse events (e.g. `MouseUp`, `MouseDown`) are signalled very rapidly?
2. What happens if a reformatted cursor moves away from the control defining the new format?

Section 5

Storyboarding

You will learn about an approach to the design of a Visual Program suitable for applications based on multiple forms.

A technique for designing the users' view of a program has been taken from film-makers. This approach, known as **storyboarding**, concentrates on the appearance of the various screens presented to users while the program is running. In this respect, there is an obvious similarity between films and Visual Programs. Both appear as a sequential set of scenes on a flat screen. Each scene may consist of a number of pictures, but will be shown from a given viewpoint. When the viewpoint changes, it is time to specify another scene.

Figure 9.10 Storyboard

A storyboard is a plan, usually on paper, showing the main aspects of the film, scene by scene. In this it very much resembles a strip cartoon, familiar from daily newspapers and comics. A number of frames hold successive parts of the action, with dialogue and explanatory comments added to suit the story. This approach is well suited to be used in the design of a Visual Program. An early draft of such a storyboard is shown in Figure 9.10, intended to show a ball being thrown for and retrieved by a dog.

There is also a significant difference. In a finished film, the audience can have no effect on the action shown. Once the film has been produced and printed for projection, it is fixed in its sequence. In a Visual Program, however, it is a normal situation for the sequence presented to the user to depend on choices made by the user. Visual Programs are typically interactive. Because of this, the corresponding storyboard may not be linear. It may have branching points and loops. In this way, it may be more typical of a flowchart.

It will therefore be subject to the strengths and weaknesses inherent in a flowchart. It is strong because it is flexible in its approach. The standard descriptions of sequence, selection and iteration may be shown; but non-standard flows of control may also be represented. These include control transfer into and out of loops and subroutines, and similar dangerous practices. These weaknesses impose the need for strong discipline on the designers of Visual Programs. However desirable it may appear to construct programs in this way, their maintenance becomes correspondingly difficult.

CRUCIAL TIP

Do not try to be 'clever' when designing Visual Programs (or any others). In the long run, it is a dangerous practice.

Thus each frame of the program design storyboard will correspond to a more-or-less static representation of a screen. Small variations within the frame will be annotated in a suitable way. Each frame can be designed, implemented and tested independently to ensure that its internal functionality is correct. The ways in which it is linked to other frames may then be organised. This is a **bottom-up** approach to the design of a Visual Program.

Alternatively, the framework of the Visual Program may be designed, implemented and tested to ensure that the transition between frames will be satisfactory. The individual frames may then be developed within this framework. This corresponds to a **top-down** approach to the design and implementation.

CRUCIAL CONCEPT

Top-down and bottom-up approaches to design are equally valid.

A suitable annotation should be associated with each transition between frames of a storyboard. This will explain the reasons for the transfer between one frame and the next, and the conditions which will apply for that transition to take place. In this respect, a storyboard resembles a State-Transition Diagram, which is used in other parts of the discipline of computing.

Each change between frames will be subject to an **event**. This event may be an input from a user, such as the use of the keyboard or the mouse, or it may come from other sources.

Such sources may be the passage of a certain amount of time, or the encounter with abnormal circumstances, such as an error. These events should be carefully considered during the time that the design is developed. The inclusion of an otherwise unforeseen event during the implementation or testing stages is unnecessarily complex, leading to significantly increased work.

The frames may use different controls according to the ways in which they are constructed and used. If the contents of the frames are simple graphics, a picture box may be used. If they are really simple, then an image control may be sufficient. The guiding approach to selecting the control is to use the one with no more than the minimum requirements which will enable the task to be carried out.

CRUCIAL TIP

Any control should be chosen to have no more functionality than it needs.

If the frames are used to carry out more complex tasks, each one may be based on a suitable form. The forms may be used cooperatively so that each nominates its successor in a well-defined manner according to the storyboard design. It may alternatively be felt better to have an overall directing form, which switches between other forms according to the requirements of the design. Either approach has its advantages and disadvantages. The application of an MDI form to organise multiple forms is particularly appropriate in this situation.

Quick test

1. What are the similarities and the differences between the top-down and the bottom-up design approaches?
2. How do event-driven programs differ from other kinds of program?

Section 6

End of chapter assessment

Questions

1. How should a simple error be detected and corrected?
2. What are the advantages of using a Multiple Document Interface?
3. Why should individual forms need to communicate in a Visual Program?
4. Why might different mouse pointer formats help in a Visual Program?
5. What advantages does storyboarding bring to Visual Program design?
6. Why is some program code developed in independent modules?
7. What is the advantage of printing a form directly from a Visual Program?
8. What extra information is provided by the mouse-based event routines?

Answers

1. Any error detection not left to the standard default treatment should be planned for and checked as soon after its possible occurrence as possible. Specific error signals should then provide useful user or Visual Program information. Real errors should be corrected automatically if possible, and otherwise referred to the user by a suitable message interface.

2. The MDI allows multiple forms to be organised efficiently under a common control. Multiple forms are useful if several different interfaces are appropriate for a Visual Program, following a storyboard approach to event-driven program design.

3. Although the interfaces supplied by different forms may appear to be separate, they all form part of the same application. The information gathered in one part of the application may be used in any other part, and this will require cooperation between separately designed subsections of the Visual Program.

4. In any application, if more information can be **efficiently** supplied to a user, it is more likely that its use will be successful. The different formats available to a cursor provide useful visual clues to users about options currently available to them, and the uses for which a Visual Program is currently enabled.

5. Because the effect of a storyboard approach breaks up the overall design into smaller parts, each part is more comprehensible. The structure and sequencing imposed by a storyboard helps in the understanding at a high level of Visual Program structure. The individual frames allow more concentration to be given to more detailed parts of the application.

6. Not all code for Visual Programs has a direct connection with controls visible to the user. Some housekeeping routines are independent of specific controls, but applicable to many of them. Such routines are organised into independent code modules for efficient storage.

7. The Visual Program allows the form to be set up and checked visually by the user. If necessary, it can be modified. It can then be printed in the knowledge that it has been implemented according to its specification.

8. The mouse event interface not only provides position information, but also the state of the mouse buttons which caused the event. At the same time, the keyboard status is described for certain keys.

Section 7

Further reading and research

There are many sources of information here. Try *http://www.vbinformation.com/ tut-mice.htm* as an example.

Chapter 10
Checking and maintaining systems

Chapter summary

Following the introduction of simple error handling, a wider view is taken, so as to provide for more robust Visual Programs. The different advantages of interpreting and compiling Visual Programs is recalled. A useful approach to the design of a Visual Program is described, and a further file-handling control is introduced. The way in which a Visual Program may be converted into a self-contained package for wider use is described.

Learning outcomes

The learning outcomes of this chapter deal with wider implications of Visual Program production. After the successful completion of this chapter, you will be able to:

Outcome 1: **Deal with generic errors in a Visual Program.**
Outcome 2: **Understand some of the differences between interpreting and compiling Visual Programs.**
Outcome 3: **Develop a framework for developing Visual Program designs.**
Outcome 4: **Use a further Visual Program control to help with file handling.**
Outcome 5: **Make a Visual Program ready for distribution to its users.**

How will you be assessed on this?

Typically you may be asked to answer questions about more general approaches to error handling, the environment in which a Visual Program is executed, and its influence on Visual Program design. You may also have to implement other file handling interfaces, and show how a working Visual Program may be prepared for distribution to its users.

Section 1

Error handling during Visual Program execution

In this section further ways are discussed to deal with errors which might arise during the execution of a Visual Program.

It is unfortunately true that all programs, and many other things, are prone to error. There is nothing that can be done about that, but a professional Visual Programmer should work hard to minimise the effect of any such errors. At the same time, any errors that do arise should be dealt with in a way which is meaningful to the user of the Visual Program. Messages should be as accurate as possible **in the user's terms**, and may usefully make suggestions about how to recover from the effects of the error, or how to avoid it in the future.

CRUCIAL TIP

Put yourself in the user's place. Do your messages make sense to a user who is not as familiar with the 'nuts and bolts' of Visual Programming as you are?

The error handling introduced in Chapter 9 used particular facilities of the Visual Program. This section will look at more general aspects. These may not have been included specifically in the program design, but they must nevertheless be dealt with.

Whenever an error is detected in a Visual Program, an error event occurs in the same way as user-generated events occur. It is therefore necessary to provide an error event handler to deal with the circumstances relating to the error. If the Visual Program does not contain an explicit error event handler, the Visual Basic system provides a default handler. However, because this has to be able to deal with any one of the very many possible errors which may occur, it has been made as simple as possible. It is therefore primitive, and gives just sufficient information to enable a programmer to carry out debugging activities before halting the Visual Program. This is quite unsatisfactory from a user's point of view.

A simple example of this interface is shown in Figure 10.1. An arithmetic calculation has taken place somewhere in the Visual Program which has involved an attempt to divide a number by zero. This is not allowed, and an error event has been generated. This event has been trapped by the default error handler, which does no more than give a simple message and offer a number of possibilities for further action. From the standpoint of a user, this is almost certainly meaningless.

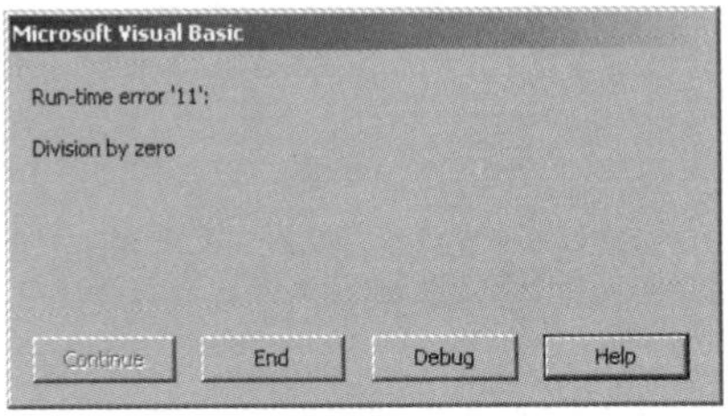

Figure 10.1 Default error report

The Visual Programming system, however, allows specific error handlers to be constructed which can give more helpful diagnostic messages. Such handlers may be changed within a Visual Program, so that the context of given problems may always be relevant.

CRUCIAL CONCEPT

A Visual Program may contain many error handlers, each carefully organised to deal with a limited number of possible errors in a highly specific way.

Associated with each error is an error number. This is an integer in the range 0 – 65535; but most common errors have associated values below 500. Two other examples of these are error 9, Subscript out of range and error 71, Disk not ready. Appropriate use of this information will enable a Visual Programmer to provide application-specific actions and messages. The value is available in the predefined variable `Err.Number`.

The error handler is specified by use of the `On Error GoTo <label>` statement, where `<label>` is a valid Visual Program identifier. This label identifier, followed by a colon, is placed immediately before the first statement of the error handler. This indicates to the Visual Program that if an error event is detected, the next statement to be obeyed should be the one following the specified label. Such a label is local in scope; that is, the label and the associated error handler must be in the same subroutine as the On Error statement. Be careful. Make sure that your error handler cannot be entered or left wrongly. If it is embedded in a subroutine, the last executable statement before the label should be End or Exit Sub, or a similar statement.

CRUCIAL TIP

It is better (just) to give too much information when an error is detected, than too little.

After the handler has taken whatever corrective action is necessary, and offered advice to the user to assist as appropriate, the main part of the program code should be re-entered; or if this is not possible, the Visual Program should be terminated. If corrective action has been taken, the error handling should finish with the Resume or the Resume Next statement. The first of these attempts the failing instruction code again, and the second carries on at the statement immediately after the one which generated the error. Which is used depends on the nature of the corrective action. Termination simply involves the End statement.

CRUCIAL ACTIVITY

Construct an error handler using a Message Box which will provide user-friendly messages, and allow the Visual Program to continue or to be shut down afterwards. Make sure that you understand the difference between the Resume and the Resume Next statements.

Quick test

1. What happens when an error is detected in a Visual Program?

2. Who is more important to a Visual Program: its developer and writer, or its user? Why?

Section 2

Interpreting and compiling

You will be reminded about the differences between interpreted code and compiled code.

The Visual Programs written so far have all been **interpreted**. That is to say, the source code has been read a fragment at a time, and each action has taken place according to the meaning of the fragment. (The fragment is usually a single line, but this is not always necessarily the case.) This has a great advantage during the development of an application. If any errors are encountered, the error can be identified in terms of the source code.

The development environment in which a Visual Program is constructed is a controlled environment. This environment is on the lookout for trouble, and is ready to assist the developer if there is a problem. It provides help in cases of doubt, and has a considerable background of resources just in case they might be needed.

Once the Visual Program has been debugged, this environment should no longer be needed. It is therefore appropriate to **compile** and link the source code into executable code, more immediately understandable to the operating system. The text which makes up the Visual Program is converted during this process into a set of machine-based instruction codes. These are directly obeyed by the instruction processor in the computer system.

One advantage of this is an increase in execution speed. At the same time, for many larger applications, there is also a decrease in overall program size. And from the point of view of security, executable code which has been compiled and linked is more difficult to change.

CRUCIAL CONCEPT

Source code is often more compact than executable code. But it carries the overhead of the interpreter which is needed for it to function. This is not the case for an executable program.

The security matter may not appear to be of great importance in general use. The author's experience is otherwise. There is nothing quite so frustrating as attempting to debug a program which has been distributed, but which has been altered subsequently.

In any case, a Visual Program intended for actual use should be compiled and linked, and all tests reapplied. It may be felt that its functionality should be unchanged. In an ideal world, this would be true. But, as suggested in earlier chapters, it is as well to be suspicious. Perhaps this Visual Program has discovered a small but important aspect of the system not so far detected, leading to an unwanted effect. Therefore, after compilation, check it all again.

This is an important step in the life of a Visual Program. It marks the point where development and debugging have finished, and all testing has been completed with satisfactory outcomes. The specifications, and any alterations which have been made to them, have all been met. If anything goes wrong, or any of the instructions are unclear, it is too late to change.

The development environment provides a rapid and easy way of compiling and linking a Visual Program when it has been fully constructed. This is described in Section 5 below.

Quick test

1. How important is an increase in the execution speed of a Visual Program?

2. Why is source code for a Visual Program generally smaller than the executable equivalent?

Section 3

Prototyping

A framework for Visual Program development will be described.

Different approaches to design have already been described. The first of these were to enable the development of single-form applications based on events. These were also extended to show how multiple-form interfaces may be described. These represent the tools used to help in the construction of a given Visual Program.

There is an assumption underlying their use. It is expected that the problem to be solved is known in sufficient detail. This is not always the case. In some instances, a more general understanding of the user's needs has been expressed, but without much of the detail which will be essential. It will not be possible to construct the final version of the application until that detail has been discovered. But it will be possible to start the construction, and to check with the user whether the assumptions made are correct. This represents the beginning of the **prototyping** approach to Visual Program design.

Once these initial ideas have been implemented and confirmed, it will be possible to ask the user further questions to clarify other parts of the implementation requirements. Note that a preliminary implementation forms part of this process. It will be acknowledged to be incomplete, but it will still be well-defined. It will be the first in a series of prototypes.

CRUCIAL CONCEPT

The users are the most important people in the life of a Visual Program.

These questions will lead in turn to a more developed Visual Program, which can again be checked for correctness with respect to the user's wishes. This process can be repeated until the full functionality and appearance required by the user has been achieved. Each prototype will be available for checking at all subsequent stages.

As should be apparent from this short description, one of the key features of this approach is the active involvement of the user. Descriptions of activities carried out and requirements needed for further development must be phrased in terms with which the user is comfortable. The right answer to the wrong question is no better than the wrong answer to the right question. It may be worse, because the user and the implementor may each believe that the construction of the Visual Program is proceeding correctly when this is not the case.

CRUCIAL TIP

Be very careful indeed to ask the correct questions, and to ensure that the user has understood the situation. Rephrase the questions, and ask again, to check. It saves a lot of time in the lifetime of even a small Visual Program.

This approach to design is well suited to Visual Programs. Based on storyboarding design, an early prototype will probably consist of the user interface, with little more. The functionality behind the interface may be artificial, and extremely small. It may be no larger than that required to show some transitions in the interface. If this approach satisfies the user, functionality can be added. But if it does not, it is better to amend it early in the development process, when such amendments are easier to carry out.

It also helps to establish confidence between the user and the implementor. Watching the progress being made to their own Visual Program according to requirements which are carefully demonstrated and discussed leads to valuable involvement. Any misconceptions or errors which might appear may be changed quickly, and this will be seen to have been done.

This does not mean that more formal ways of designing program code are not used. Prototyping typically deals with the user interface and the functionality of the Visual Program, not with its detailed coding. **What** is to be done is not the same as **how** it is to be done. Pseudocode, program structure diagrams, and other similar tools are still valuable when the program code is being constructed and tested.

Quick test

1. How should one ensure that the right path is being followed during the construction of a Visual Program?

2. Name three ways of getting information from a user.

Section 4

More file handling

The requirements to complete a more user-friendly implementation of the editor example Visual Program are introduced.

There is one control available for file handling which has not yet been introduced. This is the **file list box** control. It was mentioned at the end of Chapter 6 that the editor application would be revisited. But before formally describing the facilities offered by this control, it is important to recall another aspect of the development of a Visual Program, which appeared earlier in Chapter 6.

It is dangerous merely to add items to an existing Visual Program, and tackling the resulting issues as they arise. Far better is the approach recommended by F. P. Brooks Junior in *The Mythical Man Month*: 'Plan to throw one away'. It is much safer to go back two steps, with the lessons already learned, and go forward again from that point.

Why two steps? What are the two steps? The first one, moving backwards, is the **design** step. Rather than adding patches to the existing Visual Program, look more carefully at the basic requirements of the **specification**. That, however, is the other backwards step. If the functionality required of the Visual Program changes, this represents a change in specification, probably organised in consultation with the prospective user. It is possible that the specification as presented has not changed, but it should be checked.

─── CRUCIAL TIP ───

Better safe than sorry.

In Chapter 3, the specification was based on the details of the user interface to be supplied. This should therefore be formally respecified. To allow for all of the changes, and following the style in which this application was introduced, that user interface will form the basis of the specification. This is shown in Figure 10.2.

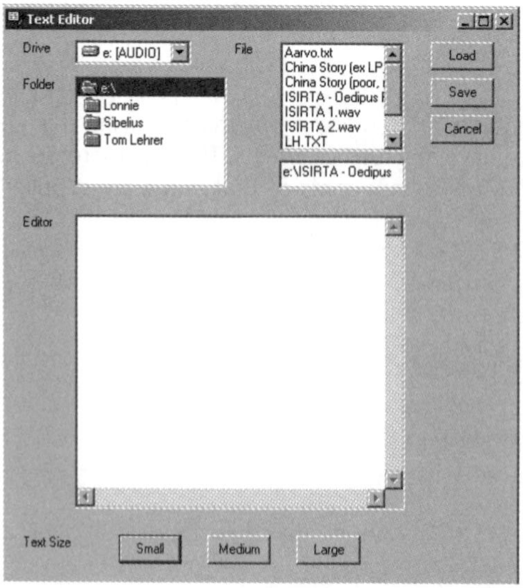

Figure 10.2 Specification by user interface

The drive list box and the directory list box are each included, with suitable label identification. The file list box has been added, with a label of *File*. The original text box, which held the complete file name, has now been resized and placed below the file list box.

The specification will now be changed to include appropriate functionality, based on the controls and other knowledge which has been introduced since the early attempt. As a user, what should be available at various times during the use of the editor? As a general approach, all controls should be visible throughout the execution of the editor, because they form an important part of its functionality.

When the application starts, there is nothing to save, so that the *Save* command button should be disabled on entry. The text size command buttons should be treated similarly. All other controls should be enabled. These aspects do not appear in Figure 10.2: that is a prototype only. These buttons should not be enabled until the text of a suitable file has been provided. This is signalled by a *Change* event associated with the editor text box.

CRUCIAL ACTIVITY

Organise a form with the controls mentioned above on it. Be sure that the appearance is similar. Rename each control according to Hungarian Notation, and set up captions to correspond to the design.

Now consider what should happen for each control. According to the principles in the early part of Chapter 6, start with the easy ones. These are the *Cancel* and the Text Size command buttons, and all of the labels. The functionality of these has not altered; so that if they are enabled, the original program code is satisfactory.

Now for the file specification controls. If a drive is selected, it should affect the folder list. If a folder is selected, it should affect the file list. If a file is selected, it should affect the file name shown in the text box. The order of those is important. For example, it should be possible to change the file name without affecting the drive or folder names. And a change in the drive name, changing the folder details, will automatically affect the file list, and thence the text box.

There are also aspects of the internal organisation which can benefit from this approach. Any of these changes should be organised to change the global variable which holds the current file name. This should be kept up to date with a single independent subroutine, called from any place which requires its effects. Because its purpose is to provide a string value whenever it is called, that of the filename, it should be made into a function.

This centralisation of all activities connected with the construction of the filename has a further advantage. If any component of that filename is input by the user, it must be checked to ensure that it is valid. If any problem arises from this, the user can be asked to correct it before it can have any further effects. This will therefore only apply to the simple filename, because all other components of that name are supplied by the system.

The filename is required in two places only, to open a file for reading, and to write a file. The function can therefore be given that information by a single parameter. Tests can be centralised to ensure that any error connected with those accesses can be trapped. The user can thus be warned about trying to read from a non-existent file. A similar warning can be given if a file is about to be overwritten, if its name differs from the original.

CRUCIAL CONCEPT

Centralisation of allied functions in a single routine is an aid to robust Visual Program design. (This is an example of strong **cohesion**.)

To check a string for validity as a filename requires that the pattern does not contain any invalid characters. These include asterisks, question marks and similar characters used for other purposes by the file system. There are two ways of checking for these, one explicit and one implicit.

In the explicit approach, illustrated in Figure 10.3, each character in the name is compared with the forbidden characters. If any one is found, the string is rejected; otherwise, it is accepted. This approach uses the Mid function, which selects a substring from within a given string starting at a specified place. In this case, as single characters are being checked, the substring has length 1. The Len function gives the number of characters in a string. This example also shows that a string differs from a list of characters. Lists have indexes running from 0, but the first character of a string is character number 1. (Note: the example is not complete: all of the possible characters have not been used; this is for illustrative purposes only.)

```
bIllegalName = False
For iCharPoint = 1 To Len(sFileName)
    sCheckChar = Mid(sFileName, iCharPoint, 1)
    If sCheckChar = "*" Or sCheckChar = "?" Then bIllegalName = True
    End If
Next iCharPoint
```

Figure 10.3 Filename character check

To use the implicit checking approach, because the checking of a string against a pattern is a common requirement, a special function has been provided. This is the Like function, and it is used as follows:

$$bIllegalName = sFileName \; Like \; "*[*?]*"$$

* represents 'any string' and characters enclosed in brackets [ ] represent any one of those present, so that the pattern is interpreted as 'any string, followed by either an asterisk or a question mark, followed by any string'. This is a powerful facility, and therefore should be accompanied by explanatory comments wherever it is used in the code of a Visual Program.

It is not intended in this text to describe the final implementation of the editor example in any greater detail. It is believed that enough information has been given for an interested participant to realise the project in full. As usual, though, this will not necessarily be an easy task, but it should be straightforward.

Quick test

1. Which property of a file list box holds the selected filename?
2. What is the advantage of centralising operations depending on a common set of parameters?

Section 5

Packaging the system

You will learn how to make a Visual Program available to its users.

When an application has been successfully designed, implemented and tested, it should be made ready for its users. It is not generally feasible for those users to have a copy of the complete Visual Basic system. Most of the facilities it provides are not appropriate for their use. Further, most of the facilities are not used by a typical application, because each application uses only a subset of the full Visual Programming facilities. For these reasons, the developed Visual Program should now be translated into an executable format. This follows from the reasons given in Section 2.

─────────────── CRUCIAL CONCEPT ───────────────
Visual Programs should not be distributed except as finished products.

So far, all of the Visual Basic instructions and programs described have been interpreted. Each line of source code has been processed and its intentions executed as it has been encountered. This makes the development and debugging of the application very much simpler. However, the translation to executable code is not a complex matter for the programmer. The *File* menu of the Visual Program Development Environment provides a *Make* option. This compiles the source code produced into computer-system executable instructions. It then formats them into an executable file, with file extension .EXE. This can be obeyed directly within the operating system, without calling on any Development Environment facilities.

The menu is shown in Figure 10.4: the *Make* option is indicated by an arrow. The Development Environment suggests a default name and folder, but these can be changed before the file is saved. There are also options to provide further information to be included in the executable program.

File	Edit	View	Project	Format	Debug	Run
New Project				Ctrl+N		
Open Project...				Ctrl+O		
Add Project...						
Remove Project						
Save Project						
Save Project As...						
Save frmEditor.frm				Ctrl+S		
Save frmEditor.frm As...						
Save Selection						
Save Change Script						
Print...				Ctrl+P		
Print Setup...						
Make Editor.exe...						
Make Project Group...						

Figure 10.4 Packaging the program

─────────────── CRUCIAL ACTIVITY ───────────────
Package one of your programs for distribution. Look at the options available, and use the associated Help file to make sure you know what can be done to help the user.

129

One more item is needed before a user can run the application. The file MSVBVM60.DLL must be available, which is usually stored in the SYSTEM folder. If it has not been provided by the operating system, it may be downloaded from any of several internet sites.

CRUCIAL TIP
Please be aware that these module and folder names are specific to the language, version and operating system in use. See Chapter 1 for the details corresponding to the approach used in this text.

It is also useful to be able to customise your product. Among other things, this allows it to be recognised more easily. A simple part of this is to include a suitable icon to identify its purpose. The most convenient way to do this is by including it on the form. This helps in two ways. The icon is then available to the operating system to identify the executable file, and appears in Windows Explorer. It also appears in the program's window frame when it is launched (in the usual position in the top left-hand corner).

CRUCIAL TIP
Customising a product is a helpful activity. But be discreet – don't 'shout'.

To customise, you need to identify a place where icons are stored. They are small bitmaps, with the file extension .ICO. If you are not sure where they might be, search the file system for files of this type. You can then select a suitable icon for use in the product. It now only remains to attach the icon to the Visual Program. This is done using the Properties menu for the program's Form. Click the Icon property, and then load the required icon using the file window shown.

Quick test

1. How is a program icon stored?
2. Why should a Visual Program be packaged for distribution?

End of chapter assessment

Questions

1. What are the disadvantages of a prototyping approach to design?
2. What are the expected functional differences between a compiled Visual Program and one which is interpreted?
3. At what point in the life cycle of a Visual Program should it be packaged for distribution?
4. Have all of the available file-handling controls now been described?
5. What are the differences between the Resume and the Resume Next statements?

Answers

1. A prototyping design should not be used if it is not possible to interact with the user or a suitable substitute. Instead, a more 'hard' approach should be used, including the specification of input and output formats and content. The actions needed to process the input to produce the output can then be defined using a method such as JSP or SSADM, suitably modified if necessary.
2. There should be no obvious functional differences between the two. Any alternative behaviour noted should be checked carefully, and reported to a suitable systems manager if verified. There are, however, non-functional differences, related to program code size and speed.

3. Packaging is **not** the last thing to be done. Once the testing of the Visual Program has been satisfactorily carried out within the design environment, it can be packaged. All the testing must then be repeated to verify that no changes have taken place in the behaviour of the Visual Program. If that is successful, the developmental part of the life cycle has finished. Corrective or adaptive maintenance may still be needed, which will lead to the need to repeat the previous steps.

4. There are other file-handling controls. An example of these is the Common Dialog control, which provides a common interface frequently used in Visual Programs for *Open* or *Save As* purposes. Check the Help files for further details.

5. The `Resume` statement assumes that any corrective action necessary has taken place so that the statement originally causing the error will now execute in a satisfactory way. The `Resume Next` statement is used if the corrective action includes provision for the functionality of the statement causing the error, so that it need not be repeated.

Section 7

Further reading and research

Brooks, Frederick P. Jr. (1979). *The Mythical Man-Month: Essays on Software Engineering*, Addison-Wesley. ISBN 0–201–00650–2.

Chapter 11
Getting the balance right

Chapter summary

Consideration of the right and wrong times to use a Visual Program is followed by a checklist of topics dealt with in the rest of the book.

Learning outcomes

The learning objectives dealt with in this chapter ensure that you can use Visual Programs in their correct context. Following its successful completion, you will be able to:

Outcome 1: Distinguish between when to use a Visual Program to solve a problem and when it is inappropriate.

Outcome 2: Extend your opportunities for learning techniques for Visual Programming.

Outcome 3: Adopt positive approaches to continuing your studies.

How will you be assessed on this?

Typically you may be asked questions about the use of Visual Programs in a wider context. For self-assessment purposes please check that you have covered the contents of this book.

Section 1

When to use a Visual Program

You will be invited to reflect on the best way of solving a problem.

Now that you have arrived at this point in the book, you have more possibilities available to you when solving problems. Before you started, you knew about at least one computer-based procedural language. You now know another one, or at least a particular way of approaching problems which was not there before.

All of the work done so far in this book expects that the problem to be addressed should use a Visual Program to solve it. Not every problem is like that. Some things to be done need no visual user interface, and would suffer if one were used. In other cases it may be optional, but should not be used just because it is there. A fast car does not need a model in the rear window with eyes that light up to help its performance. Remember KISS.

Another phrase that applies is 'Horses for courses'. This means that if you have a horse-race to run, choose a fast horse; but if the race is a steeplechase, your horse must be able to jump. The same applies to programs. If their efficiency and usefulness will benefit from being a **Visual** Program, then visual functionalities should be included. If the application is less likely to fail if its user has a friendly interface to work with, it should be a Visual Program.

Not all applications need a visual user interface. The scheduler that organises how the programs in the computer system should run does not need one. It would, in fact, be worse with one. Therefore, consider carefully when a problem comes along whether it would be better organised with – or without – such an interface.

Is it interactive? Does it need particular directions from its user? Is its information output graphical? If the answers are 'yes', the way of solving the problem is probably based on a Visual Program. Is the output printed? Does it get its data mostly from existing files? Is it highly repetitive in nature? If the answers to those questions are 'yes', the solution mechanism would probably be best approached in some other way. But if you can apply the WYSIWYG ('what you see is what you get') approach, there is a strong implication that you are seeing something. It will therefore almost certainly be based on a Visual Program.

This discussion has ignored a more fundamental question. Does the problem need a computer system in its solution at all? Such a question is always worth checking. There are many problems which have computer-based solutions which should never have been tackled this way at all. If problems are small, and can be satisfactorily organised using pencil and paper, it is usually better not to use a computer system. The strengths of computer-based solutions are greatest when the resulting programs are used many times, or are extremely repetitive in nature.

Quick test

1. What kind of program should be used for printing cheques for a payroll?

2. What kind of interface should the computers in a 'fruit machine' use?

What have you done?

This is a reminder of what has been done in this book and an opportunity to check whether you remember the topics.

Have you been keeping notes? According to the plan, some aspects of Visual Programming have been studied during this book. This has not been done exhaustively by any means, because a full treatment would need a book at least five or six times as large as this one. Some of the aspects studied are common to all programming languages, with which you should already have had some experience – look back to Chapter 1. But others are specific to Visual Programming, and to Visual Basic in particular.

The programming language topics covered, in either greater or lesser detail, are shown in Figure 11.1. These are not described in full, but are rather intended to act as a checklist. If there are any items or concepts there which do not appear in your notes, check the chapter contents. If the ideas are not familiar, this is the right time to do something about it.

--- CRUCIAL TIP ---

If you find anything which is worth following up, the first thing to do is to make a note about it. That way you will not forget it, and will be able to deal with it if you do not have time to do so at this very moment.

Some of the items not covered can be worked out from reference to what has already been done. As a simple example of that, Left and Mid, for string manipulation, were introduced in Chapters 6 and 10. There is a similar method, Right, which looks at the rightmost parts of strings. The help files are useful to check items of this kind. Their *See*

Also entries can often give useful clues about what else is available to an interested programmer.

```
ChapterTopic
1    Sub, Print, (comment), End Sub
3    Do While, Loop
     Open, Input, Close
     Dim
     (String concatenation)
5    If, Then, ElseIf, Else, End If
     For, To, Step, Next
     (Simple arithmetic), Int
     Cls
6    Left
7    Write, Case, With, End With
8    Call, Load Picture, While, Wend
9    PrintForm, (code modules)
     On Error Resume Next
10   Resume, Resume Next
     Mid, Like
```

Figure 11.1 Programming language topics

CRUCIAL ACTIVITY

Check the keywords given in Figure 11.1. Classify each one as **known**, **seen** or **unknown**. Take appropriate action for the keywords in each category.

The controls which are specific to Visual Programs have been similarly summarised in Figure 11.2, and should be approached in the same way. They have not been described in complete detail, but enough of their characteristics should have been introduced to allow you to carry on from this point. You should be able to call on the help of manuals both on-line and off-line to extend the information you already have.

```
ChapterTopic
3    Command button, Form
     Label, Text box
5    Check box, Frame
     Lines and figures, Option button
     Scroll bar, Slider
6    Directory list box, Drive list box
7    Input box, Message box
8    Combo box, Image
     List box, Picture box
     [Enable, Visible]
9    MDI Form
     [MouseUp, MouseDown, MouseMove]
     [MousePointer]
10   File list box
```

Figure 11.2 Visual Programming topics

It is worth being reminded about the power available using the internet. There are several sites which give more information about Visual Programming in general and Visual Basic in particular. This information ranges from specific points about controls and items of programming interest to sequence of program code designed to illustrate some of the applications which can form part of Visual Programs.

CRUCIAL CONCEPT

When trying to extend your knowledge, look in several places.

Quick test

1. What parameters does the `Right` method require?
2. What are the typical links at the head of each Visual Basic help page?

Section 3

What comes next?

You will be reminded about the need for continuing practice and to maintain a balance between your various activities.

This is not the end, even though you are close to the end of the book. If you are going to become a producer of Visual Programs you need to attend to two definite aspects of your craft. The first aspect is to consolidate what you already have. You need to practise the skills and reinforce the knowledge that have been introduced in this book. If you do not, you will lose what you have gained so far.

It is important not only to become fit but also to keep in training if you want to do well at sports. This is as true with these skills and knowledge as with any athletic activity. If you set aside some time each day to practise aspects you already know you will continue to improve. A well-known musician has said: 'If I don't practise for one day, **nobody** notices. If I don't practise for two days, **I** notice. If I don't practise for three days, **everybody** notices.' That is an effective approach.

Keep a balance between all of the different activities you need to carry out. The old advertisement said: 'Not too little, not too much, but just right'. If you do too little, you will lose what you already have. If you do too much, you will deprive other parts of your activities of the attention they deserve. Decide where you want to succeed and follow those pieces of advice.

The achievement of success will need planning. Keep a careful record of what you do for a week, and review it at the end of the week. Decide which of the activities deserve more time, or need less time. If you identify some aspects that can be left out, that will automatically allow more time for other more important ones. This may not be an easy process, but it will pay off. But to make this approach work properly, you must not try to fool yourself. If you do not like some of the answers you find, there may be an important message in that. There is always the opportunity to learn more about oneself.

The other aspect to look at is extending your knowledge and associated skills. Therefore, the time taken to practise Visual Programming should introduce new parts of the language system as well as consolidate ones already met. There are many books to help with this. There are also the help facilities of the Development Environment. You will need to approach both of these with a little care.

Make sure that the version of the language which you are using corresponds to the book you are using. Otherwise, you will need to be aware of inevitable differences. Much of the background for this book has originated in previous work carried out using version 3 of Visual Basic. The books used to support that work do not appear in the reading lists. There are too many detailed language differences, although the fundamental concepts remain.

Similar comments apply, perhaps surprisingly, to the information from the help files. In every case it has been necessary to check the detailed information given. It does not always correspond directly to the expected behaviour of the actual system, although it has never been wildly inaccurate. Nevertheless, it has proved a good starting point in every instance.

Quick test

1. What are the **three** most important activities you wish to maintain?

2. You know how many minutes there are in a day. How many hours are there in a week?

Section 4

And finally...

Here are some pathways and pointers to the next steps, and a *bon voyage*.

There are other languages used for Visual Programming. Among these are C++, Java and FoxPro. They share typical interface approaches, but each is naturally expressed in its own terms for communication with and through those interfaces. Some of the ideas presented in this book carry over in a straightforward way. Others have been changed to conform to the requirements of the background and development environment of the specific language.

According to your previous experience, you can take advantage of these. For instance, if you are familiar with Java, then the extension of your expertise to Visual Java should be feasible. You will need to be well aware of the similarities and differences. Carefully kept notes are of invaluable assistance for this purpose. The first and second programming languages are the hardest to deal with. The later ones become much easier to learn and apply.

Good luck: this is only the start of an interesting journey through Visual Programming. G. K. Chesterton said: 'For there is good news yet to hear and fine things to be seen, / Before we go to Paradise...'. That positive approach is the best one. Do your best to gain enjoyment from the work you do. It helps the learning and understanding processes.

Quick test

1. Does another language you already know support a visual approach?

2. How many computer languages do you know now?

Section 5

End of chapter assessment

Questions

1. Suggest one problem that should be solved using a Visual Program and one that should not. Give reasons for your choices.

2. Have you reviewed your work recently?

3. Have you looked for further sources?

Answers

1. There are, of course, many that fall into each category and some that are ambiguous. The guiding principle should be based on KISS and Occam's razor. Do you need to see what you are doing? A good example for Visual Program solution is a word processor. You can see what is happening and a good one will work on the WYSIWYG principle. As a non-visual approach, consider a music CD player. That can be dealt with entirely by loading the CD and using the keyboard. (Why are Visual Programs provided as interfaces for most CD music players?) A 'should not' example is a cheque printing program. That needs no interference and should work from existing files only.

2. There is no definite answer to this question. The answer should of course be 'Yes', but you have to be absolutely honest about the answer. It should also be qualified with 'and I've taken notes about it'. That is another powerful way to assist the memorising process.

3. A similar response applies. This book is too small to do more than introduce the topics illustrated. For best results, you must not only practise the work, but look at what others suggest. Larger books may have complete illustrative programs. Do you learn from these? If so, how? Learning is best carried out actively, not passively.

Section 6

Further reading and research

http://msdn.microsoft.com/vbasic/ will provide the basis of some World-Wide Web-based research.

Chesterton, G. K. (1913). *The Rolling English Road*, New Witness. Reprinted in *Poems For All Purposes*, Pimlico, 1994. ISBN 0–7126–5881–5.

Index